Vegan
CHRISTMAS
COOKIES
& COCOA

T0019110

AUDREY DUNHAM

Vegan CHRISTMAS COOKIES & COCOA

*Holiday treats and warm winter drinks,
all astonishingly egg and dairy-free!*

EXPANDED SECOND EDITION

DEDICATION & SPECIAL THANKS

This book is dedicated to the five Dunham kids. May your kitchens always be filled with cookies at Christmastime.

Mom, thank you for teaching me at a very young age how to follow recipes, measure properly and give cookies abundantly.

Jeff, your love and encouragement is everything. I thank you with all my heart.

Lastly, a very special thanks to my cookie and cocoa taste testers: Jeff, Jack, James, Mom, Dad, Emily, Tim, Ashlyn, and Berta. Oh yes - and to our little dog, Roadie, who helped with floor crumb cleanup!

Copyright 2021 by Audrey Dunham.
All rights reserved.

Published by Audrey Dunham Celebrations™, an imprint of Audrey Dunham, Inc.

The scanning, uploading, and distribution of this book without permission is a theft of the author's intellectual property. If you would like permission to use materials from this book (other than for review purposes) please contact audrey@audreydunham.com. Thank you for your support of the author's rights.

Audrey Dunham Celebrations™

Audrey Dunham Celebrations™

13801 Ventura Blvd.
Sherman Oaks, California 91423
www.AudreyDunham.com

Instagram and Facebook: @AudreyDunham

First Published November 2020
Expanded Second Edition November 2021

Book cover and design: Nikki Ellis
Food photography: Vanessa Stump
Food styling and prop styling: Vanessa Stump, Audrey Dunham and Chris Hatcher
Editing: Christine McKnight
Indexing: Rudy Leon
Enhancements: Matt McNeil

ISBNs: 978-1-7367601-0-9 (hardcover)
987-1-7367601-3-0 (ebook)
Library of Congress Control Number: 2021914275

Names: Dunham, Audrey, author.

Title: Vegan Christmas cookies & cocoa : holiday treats and warm winter drinks, all astonishingly egg and dairy-free! / Audrey Dunham.

Other Titles: Vegan Christmas cookies and cocoa

Description: Second edition. | Sherman Oaks, California : Audrey Dunham Celebrations, an imprint of Audrey Dunham, Inc., 2021. | Includes index.

Identifiers: ISBN 9781736760109 (hardcover) | ISBN 9781736760130 (ebook)

Subjects: LCSH: Christmas cooking. | Vegan cooking. | Cookies. | Chocolate drinks. | LCGFT: Cookbooks.

Classification: LCC TX739.2.C45 D86 2021 (print) | LCC TX739.2.C45 (ebook) | DDC 641.5686--dc23

CONTENTS

INTRODUCTION

There's just something about Christmas cookies that makes the holiday season feel especially magical. After all, they star in so many of our Christmas rituals throughout the month of December as we count down to the twenty-fifth.

FIRST, THERE'S THE BAKING. Whether you like to bake on your own or with family and friends, just put on some holiday music, gather your ingredients—flour, sugar, sprinkles, and all—and let the merriment begin!

Growing up, my mom and I usually planned one day in December to make all of our cookies. We'd pick five or so recipes—many of which have since been "veganized" and are in this book—and would have a nonstop baking marathon from morning to night until all the treats were made and decorated. We had a blast, and it soon became an annual tradition.

Just before my nineteenth birthday, my parents moved to Dallas, Texas, while I stayed behind in Southern California. I wanted to continue the one-day-a-year cookie-baking tradition on my own, but since finances were tight, I had to buy the necessary ingredients a little at a time each week, until I finally had everything I needed to make all my cookie recipes. It was so much fun, and no matter the size of my kitchen (I moved a lot!) I always managed to find space to complete every batch in one day, even if it meant allowing cookies to cool on top of my boxy television.

As the years went on, many things changed: My husband, Jeff, and I married in 2012, and I became a stepmom to Jeff's lovely daughters, Bree, Ashlyn, and Kenna. My parents moved back to Southern California in 2013, and my twin boys, Jack and James, were born in 2015. But no matter what, throughout the years, each and every December there were Christmas cookies. Sometimes I'd bake them on my own, other times with Bree, Ashlyn, or Kenna there to help decorate. These days, I most often bake with my boys, usually with Jeff or my parents somewhere nearby to help out, take photos, and make sure Jack and James don't feed the cookie dough to our dog, Roadie.

Now that Bree and her husband Eric have brought baby Harrison into the world, I know there are many more years of Christmas cookie-baking memories to be made, as our family continues to grow.

THEN, THERE'S THE GIVING. Once all the cookies are baked, there's the joy of picking out festive plates, boxes, and tins, beautifully arranging the cookies, adding the finishing touch of a red or green ribbon, and giving the cookies away as gifts.

When I was a kid, we gave plates of Christmas cookies to our neighbors, friends, and family members. My mom often sent me out to deliver the cookies, and I'll never forget the looks on our neighbors' faces as they opened the door and I handed them a plate of homemade holiday deliciousness, complete with gift tag and bow. They were so happy and surprised, they were often left nearly speechless.

Jeff and I still gift cookies to our loved ones every year, and nothing has changed—they still bring every bit as much joy as they did when I was a kid. I've seen gifts of all types and monetary values exchanged between friends and colleagues. But nothing, and I mean nothing, lights a person's face up like a gift that was made in the kitchen. If there's one lesson I hope to pass on to my kids, it's this: The best holiday gifts aren't purchased, they're homemade.

FINALLY, OF COURSE, THERE'S THE EATING! One important thing to keep in mind as you plan your Christmas cookie baking: make sure you have enough to give away, and enough to keep for yourself, too! This is something that almost goes without saying, as I know there'd be a riot in our house if I spent an entire day filling our home with the glorious sights and smells of cookies, only to give every last one of them away. I'm betting this would be the case in your home, too. After all, it's Christmas cookies we're talking about! I usually bake enough to last us until New Year's or so, as many of us aren't entirely ready to say goodbye to that joyful Christmas feeling come December twenty-sixth.

Packing up some Christmas cookies to take along is the perfect way to make all your holiday activities even more festive for you and your loved ones. This is where the hot cocoa and winter lattes enter the picture, too, as Christmas cookies and warm winter drinks are truly a sweet match made in heaven!

We like to take our cookies and cocoa in the car with us as we go for evening drives to look at Christmas lights. We also enjoy them while waiting in anticipation during tree-lighting ceremonies, or while out holiday present shopping, especially since Christmas treats are a brilliant way to keep the kids happy.

But mostly, we nibble on our Christmas cookies and sip on our warm cocoas and lattes at home. Whether we're decorating the tree, wrapping presents, or snuggling on the couch watching Christmas movies, there's nothing quite like a homemade holiday treat in one hand and a warm drink in the other to make each moment feel that much more special.

My sincerest wish for you is that this cookbook evokes the excitement of the Christmas season, and inspires you to create new Christmas baking traditions and special memories of your own, this year and every year after.

TIPS FOR MAKING PERFECT TREATS

Before starting any recipe, it's best to create your *mise en place* (MEEZ ahn plahs), which is a French term for having all your ingredients prepped and measured out into separate bowls. Mixing bowls, tools, and equipment should be set out as well. Taking the time to do this before you start baking or cooking ensures that you'll have the correct amount of each ingredient, and helps make the treat- or cookie-making process easier and more fluid once you begin.

For the most accurate ingredient measuring, I recommend using a food scale for all dry ingredients used in quantities of 1 tablespoon and up. As you'll see, I included grams as well as cup measurements in this cookbook. But since cup measurements can vary ever so slightly depending on how tightly a measuring cup is packed or how densely an ingredient sits in its package, the only true way to know if you're adding the intended amount is by weighing. The extra bonus is, your cleanup will be minimal; in the end you'll have just one bowl to wash vs. several dirty measuring cups!

If you choose to use measuring cups, I recommend using the scoop-and-sweep method for all powdery dry ingredients such as flour, powdered (confectioners') sugar, and cocoa powder. For this method, first use a fork or whisk to fluff up the top layers of the ingredient within the package to help loosen it before measuring, then take your measuring cup and scoop out a heaping amount. Using the back flat edge of a table knife or a very straight index finger, level off the top so it is even with the perimeter of the cup.

Avoid baking on warm or hot baking sheets, as this may affect the outcome of your cookies and treats. This goes for baking sheets that were just used in the oven as well as those sitting on top of the oven as it preheats. Unless otherwise noted, room-temperature baking sheets are best and will help ensure your treats come out perfectly.

For perfectly soft cookies with chewy edges, keep in mind it's better to slightly underbake than to overbake. In the past, many of us were taught to look for browned edges to know when cookies were done. But for soft cookies, you want to look for matte surfaces, rather than shiny or wet-looking ones, instead of for browning. Even if the cookies don't initially hold together when they're removed from the oven, they will likely firm up as they sit on the baking sheet for a couple of minutes. You'll see that I mention this many times throughout this book, especially in recipes where I feel aiming for softer cookies is best.

When it comes to storing cookies and other treats, I find that some store best in airtight containers, some in non-airtight containers, and some maintain the right texture either way (I've noted my recommendations at the bottom of each recipe for your convenience.) Regardless of whether or not your treats are kept in airtight containers, it's always best to allow cookies to cool completely before storing. Then, keep them away from heat (such as from a stove) and direct sunlight, unless otherwise noted in the recipe.

LET'S TALK INGREDIENTS

When it comes to vegan (dairy-free) butter or margarine, I prefer one that has "vegetable oil" or "vegetable oil blend" listed as the first ingredient rather than "coconut oil." The overall flavor and texture of vegetable oil–based butter seems to work better in the recipes. In addition, I always use butters that are salted rather than unsalted. If your butter doesn't state whether it's salted on the front of the package, simply look to the ingredients to make sure salt is listed. However, if you only have unsalted butter on hand, I recommend adding an additional ¼ tsp. of salt for every ½ cup of unsalted butter called for in the recipe.

To soften your butter more quickly for use, try this method: slice or scoop your butter by the tablespoon and place the 1-tablespoon pieces into a microwave-safe bowl, separating the pieces as much as possible from one another. Heat in the microwave for just 10 seconds. If your butter is still cold, heat for another 5 seconds. This should do the trick! Another method is to grate sticks or large mounds of butter on the largest holes of a grater and then allow it to sit at room temperature on a plate or in a bowl until soft.

Every now and then, I call for oil in this book. When it comes to choosing which type to use, I recommend using neutral-flavored oils such as canola, safflower, or sunflower, to name a few. Refrain from using coconut oil unless otherwise noted in the recipe.

If you'd like to make your cookies and treats gluten-free, look at the bottom of each recipe to see my recommendations on how to go about it. Oftentimes, the best method is simply swapping out regular all-purpose flour for gluten-free all-purpose flour. My personal preference and recommendation is to use a gluten-free all-purpose flour blend that lists garbanzo bean (chickpea) flour as the first ingredient and also includes at least one type of starch in the ingredients. But feel free to try using whichever type of gluten-free all-purpose flour you like best.

Oat flour is used in a handful of recipes in this cookbook, but it can sometimes be difficult to find in stores. Thankfully, oat flour can be easily made at home by blending old-fashioned rolled oats or quick-cooking oats in a blender or food processor until they take on the texture and look of flour. If you'd prefer to leave out the oat flour altogether, in most cases it can be replaced with extra all-purpose flour or wheat flour.

If you'd like to use whole-grain or bean flours in these recipes, in most cases, one-quarter to one-third of the all-purpose flour called for can be replaced with flours such as wheat, oat, or garbanzo bean (chickpea). Keep in mind that this may affect the color, flavor, and texture of the treats—but sometimes in a good way.

When it comes to almond and coconut flour, I don't typically recommend using either one as an all-purpose flour swap. The higher fat content of these flours can sometimes negatively affect the end result by changing the texture of the treats.

Dairy-free chocolate chips can sometimes be hard to find, so for most recipes in this cookbook, chocolate chips can be replaced with chocolate chunks or chopped chocolate bar. I recommend tasting all chocolate before using it in your recipes to make sure you like the flavor. The flavor of unpleasant-tasting chocolate can't be hidden in cookies or other treats and will come through in the end result.

When choosing candies and sprinkles for decorating, look for those free of confectioners' glaze, also known as shellac or pharmaceutical glaze, as it is made from the secretions of lac bugs and is therefore not considered vegan. This ingredient is used to give candy a shiny look, but thankfully more and more candy companies are looking to other ways to achieve this shine without using confectioners' glaze.

Red food coloring can be made in various ways, but if you want to ensure that the type you use is vegan, avoid colorings that include E120, natural red 4, cochineal extract, crimson lake, carmine lake, or C.I. 75470, as all of these ingredients indicate that the coloring was created by extracting and treating a pigment from female cochineal insects. To play it safe, check labels for shades of pinks, oranges, and purples as well as reds when choosing your food coloring.

For a list of my favorite ingredient brands, please visit: AudreyDunham.com/Ingredients

MY FAVORITE KITCHEN EQUIPMENT AND TOOLS

FOR EVERYDAY BAKING

FOOD SCALE

In the "Tips for Making Perfect Treats" section at the beginning of this cookbook, I explain why I prefer weighing all dry ingredients as opposed to using measuring cups. In a nutshell, weighing is absolutely the most accurate way to go, and it helps minimize cleanup, too. At this point, I can easily say my food scale is one of my most used and most loved kitchen tools!

METAL MEASURING CUPS FOR DRY INGREDIENTS

Although I prefer a food scale, occasionally in those moments when I quickly need a cup of nuts, oats, or chocolate chips, for example, it's just as easy to grab a measuring cup to measure instead. When it comes to measuring cups, I feel any metal type, such as stainless steel or copper, is superior to the plastic or silicone types, as I find that ingredients (especially dry, powdery ones) are less likely to stick to metal cups.

ANGLED LIQUID MEASURING CUP

Sure, just about any liquid measuring cup with legible numbers will get the job done, but I prefer using angled liquid measuring cups in my kitchen. The angled type lets you read measurements easily and effortlessly from above, which is much better than having to squat down or bend over to see if you have the right amounts!

METAL MEASURING SPOONS

A set of measuring spoons is a must for any home baker or cook, as there's hardly a recipe that does't include at least one spoon-measured ingredient. Once again, I prefer the metal type for the same reason I prefer metal measuring cups—less sticking. And if those metal measuring spoons are double-sided with one circular end and one oval-shaped end, I'm even happier! Not only can you use double-sided spoons twice before needing to wash or wipe them clean, but those oval ends tend to fit nicely into small spice bottles.

GLASS OR STAINLESS STEEL MIXING BOWLS

A set of at least two glass or stainless steel bowls is another must for any home baker or cook. I use the glass type if I want easy cleanup after baking (hello, dishwasher!), and I use the stainless steel type when baking with small kids since they won't break if they happen to slide off the counter.

STAND MIXER WITH PADDLE, WHISK, AND DOUGH HOOK ATTACHMENTS

When it comes to heavy-duty jobs such as mixing thick gingerbread dough, making larger batches of any cookie dough, whipping up perfect royal icing or homemade marshmallows, and kneading bread doughs (like those in my cookbook Vegan Thanksgiving Dinner and Pies), it's hard to beat a solid stand mixer.

5-SPEED HANDHELD MIXER

For simpler jobs such smaller batches of cookies or making homemade whipped cream, I always turn to my lightweight and easy-to-use handheld mixer. In fact, I still own and use the same mixer I purchased at eighteen years old when I moved into my first apartment!

FOOD PROCESSOR

Food processors are wonderful for completing recipe tasks including blending, crushing, shredding, and chopping in just a few seconds. I feel as though I'm constantly finding new uses for mine! What's nice is that once you own one, it will typically last for many years, if not decades.

RUBBER SPATULA WITH A THIN EDGE

A rubber spatula, also sometimes called a scraper, is the go-to utensil for such tasks as scraping every last bit from a bowl without scratching the surface, blending batters and other mixtures, and gently folding ingredients into mixtures. I especially love using mine to transfer brownie batter or homemade marshmallow mixture to a baking dish, or to remove royal icing from a mixing bowl.

ROLLING PIN

When rolling dough for cutout cookies such as sugar cookies, linzers, or gingerbread folks, the perfect tool is a good ol' rolling pin. I prefer the type that has handles on either end, but any type will do!

COOKIE CUTTERS

When it comes to choosing cookie cutters for cutout cookies, I prefer the metal type. Since their edges are typically super thin and somewhat sharp, metal cutters create nice clean cuts in the cookie dough.

PRECUT UNBLEACHED PARCHMENT PAPER SHEETS

These are truly one of the best inventions ever! Lining your baking sheets with parchment paper means you'll have an easier time cleaning up at the end of the day. When you purchase the flat, precut type, you won't need to worry about the edges curling up on you, as often happens with parchment paper purchased in rolls.

For a list of my favorite brands for kitchen equipment and tools, please visit: AudreyDunham.com/KitchenTools

BAKING SHEETS

My baking sheets are another kitchen tool that I use almost daily. I prefer the half-sheet size (also called a half-sheet pan), which measure 18 x 13 inches (about 46 x 33 cm) with sides about 1 inch (about 3 cm) high. I recommend home bakers and cooks keep at least two baking sheets on hand for all of their baking (and vegetable roasting!) needs.

2-QUART AND 3-QUART BAKING DISHES

For baking brownies, blondies, pecan pie bars, or any other type of bar treat, perfectly square or rectangular-shaped baking pans are a must. In this cookbook, I call for two different sizes: a 2-quart dish such as an 8-x-8-inch (about 20-x-20-cm) square pan, and a 3-quart dish such as a 9-x-13-inch (about 23-x-33-cm) pan. Both glass and most metal dishes work well, as long as the sides are at least 2 inches (about 5 cm) high and they're properly greased according to the recipe instructions.

METAL SPATULA

A thin metal spatula is definitely the ideal tool for removing cookies from a baking sheet. Metal spatulas slide under the cookies easily without incident, as opposed to some thicker plastic spatulas that can cause cookies to bunch up or break apart.

COOLING RACKS

There are two things I look for in a cooling rack: sturdiness and a perfectly flat surface. If a cooling rack in a store appears to be bent, uneven, or wobbly while standing, it never makes it to the checkout stand with me! It's best to have at least two cooling racks in your kitchen for cooling cookies and pans filled with bar treats such as brownies.

SAUCEPANS

Whether you're making the filling for date bars or warming milk for hot cocoa, a saucepan is a must for warming soft or liquid ingredients on the stove. I'd say a 2-quart saucepan is the safest size if you were to purchase just one, but 1-quart and 3-quart sizes will come in handy as well. Any type will do, just so long as the handle has a nice grip, it's a weight you're comfortable with, and it comes with a lid.

FOR SLIGHTLY ADVANCED BAKING

COOKIE PRESS

A good cookie press is needed to create spritz cookies, with their signature fun shapes and designs. I wish I could say that any cookie press will do, but sadly not all cookie presses are created equal. Jump online and find one with numerous high ratings. Spending a couple extra dollars for a good cookie press could mean the difference between spritz cookies that turn out versus those that do not.

PIPING BAGS AND TIPS

When it comes to decorating cookies with royal icing, you'll need a piping bag fitted with a round decorating tip in size 2 or 3 to ensure success. These are inexpensive and much easier to use than a resealable plastic storage bag with the corner cut off! Save yourself the frustration and opt for piping bags with tips instead. If you'd like to use more than one size piping tip while decorating without having to use a whole new piping bag, fit your bag with a coupler first so you can easily swap out the tips.

RETRACTABLE SCOOPS

A set of retractable scoops of various sizes can certainly come in handy when measuring truffles; portioning out cookie doughs that are sticky, loose, or crumbly; or making cookies that need to be an exact size. I have a set of five scoops that range from ½ Tbsp. (25 mm) in size all the way up to 4 Tbsp. (56 mm), and I use them regularly. Aside from measuring truffle fillings and cookie dough, they also work marvelously in creating melon or other fruit balls, forming balls of butter to set out at the dining room table, and measuring out batter for muffins and cupcakes. Oh yes, and of course for scooping ice cream, too!

MY FAVORITE NON-DAIRY MILKS FOR BAKING

Gone are the days of soy as the only non-dairy milk choice! At this point in time, there are countless non-dairy milks made from a variety of plant-based foods. I will say, however, when it comes to using them in baking, there are some that I prefer over others.

In my experience, the milks that work best in baking recipes are those that have low to moderate amounts (about 4 grams or less per 1 cup / 237 ml) of fats and carbohydrates. For example, although oat milk is a big favorite among non-dairy milk drinkers and I certainly love it too, it typically contains high amounts of both carbohydrates, from the oats, and fats, from the oil usually added by the manufacturer. The quantity of carbs and fats in this type of milk can negatively affect the results of a baking recipe, altering the texture and look of the finished product.

A higher amount of of protein, on the other hand, as in soy milk for example, doesn't seem to negatively affect the results of a recipe. In fact, higher amounts of protein can be helpful with recipes that require a lot of structure, mainly cakes and breads. I would, however, avoid using milks with high amounts of added protein, to play it safe.

When it comes down to it, my preference for baking is an unsweetened (or lightly sweetened), unflavored almond, cashew, or soy milk containing 25–70 calories per 1 cup (237 ml). The calorie count is a nice and easy number to check, as any number higher than 70 usually indicates the milk is high in carbs and/or fats.

For those who have allergies to both nuts and soy, my fourth choice at this point in time is a low-fat oat milk. It may be higher in carbohydrates, but at least it's lower in fats.

MY FAVORITE NON-DAIRY MILKS FOR HOT COCOA AND LATTES

When choosing a non-dairy milk for hot cocoa, there is only one type I avoid: oat milk that has added omega-3s. This pains me to say, because omega-3s are an essential fat that almost all of us need to consume more of, but the source of the omega-3s added to oat milk is usually algae oil. While I encourage you to consume algae oil for its omega-3s in any other circumstance, when hot or warm, this oil can make oat milk taste like the ocean (aka fishy). This, of course, can completely ruin your hot cocoas and lattes.

My top non-dairy milk choice for hot beverages is the same as my preference for baking: unsweetened (or lightly sweetened), unflavored almond, cashew, or soy milk. If we're talking iced lattes or coffee, though, then omega-3-spiked oat milk is a top choice! The added algae oil is undetectable when the milk is cold.

CHRISTMAS COOKIES

SALTED CARAMEL TURTLE COOKIES

Soft chocolate cookies covered in creamy caramel and topped with toasted pecans and a sprinkle of salt . . . Yes, these cookies are as good as (if not better than) you can imagine.

YIELD: **12 COOKIES**

INGREDIENTS:
Cookies:
- 1 Tbsp. (8 g) ground flaxseed
- 2 Tbsp. (30 ml) water
- ⅔ c. (93 g) all-purpose flour
- ¼ c. (27 g) oat flour
- ½ c. (115 g) granulated sugar
- ¼ c. (54 g) packed brown sugar
- ⅓ c. (27 g) cocoa powder
- ½ tsp. salt + more for topping
- ½ tsp. baking powder
- ⅓ c. + 1 Tbsp. (94 ml) oil
- 1 tsp. vanilla extract
- 3 Tbsp. (24 g) pecans, finely chopped

Date Caramel Sauce:
- ½ c. (115 g) dates, pitted and roughly chopped
- ⅓ c. (79 ml) non-dairy milk
- ¼ c. (59 ml) maple syrup
- 3 Tbsp. (41 g) vegan butter or margarine
- ½ tsp. vanilla extract

FOR BEST GLUTEN-FREE VERSION:
Try your favorite gluten-free all-purpose flour in place of the regular all-purpose flour. Check the labels for all remaining ingredients to ensure they're gluten-free, as well.

INSTRUCTIONS:
1. Preheat your oven to 350°F (approx. 177°C). In a small bowl, combine the ground flaxseed and water and set aside.
2. Using a handheld or stand mixer, combine the flours, sugars, cocoa powder, salt, and baking powder on low speed.
3. Add the oil, vanilla extract, and the ground flaxseed mixture to the dry ingredients and mix again on low until just combined.
4. Using your hands, gather the dough into one big ball, then create twelve 1 ½-inch (4-cm) dough balls and place them on parchment-lined or ungreased baking sheet(s) 3 inches (7 cm) apart from one another. Using the palm of your hand, flatten each ball ever so slightly.
5. Bake the cookies in your preheated oven for 12–13 minutes or until the surface of the cookies is matte rather than shiny. The tops may be slightly domed, but that's okay; they'll flatten as they cool. Leave the oven on. Allow the cookies to cool on the baking sheet for 2–3 minutes before transferring to a cooling rack.
6. Meanwhile, place the chopped pecans on a baking sheet and toast in the oven for 3 minutes. Remove from the oven and set aside.
7. To prepare the caramel, combine all the ingredients in a blender and blend until very smooth.
8. Once the cookies are completely cool, spread a generous amount of caramel over the top of each one. Then sprinkle with the toasted pecans, followed by a light pinch of salt.

STORAGE:
These cookies are best stored in airtight containers or on plates covered in plastic wrap.

CHERRY THUMBPRINT COOKIES

These cherry thumbprint cookies are truly irresistible with their festive, bright red cherries and white chocolate drizzle. Perfect for parties or cookie tins, as they are loved by kids and adults alike! (Just ask any member of my family.)

YIELD: 16 COOKIES

INGREDIENTS:
- ½ c. + 1 Tbsp. (129 g) cold vegan butter or margarine
- ½ c. + 1 Tbsp. (127 g) granulated sugar
- 1 ½ tsp. vanilla extract
- 1 tsp. almond extract
- 1 ½ c. (210 g) all-purpose flour
- 1 tsp. cornstarch
- ¼ tsp. salt
- 1 (10 oz. / 300 g) can or jar cherry pie filling*
- ½ c. (about 78 g) vegan white chocolate discs, chips, or chopped white chocolate bar

*Can't find cherry pie filling? Preserves or jam will work as well— the brighter red, the better.

FOR BEST GLUTEN-FREE VERSION:
Try using your favorite gluten-free all-purpose flour in place of the regular all-purpose flour. Check the labels for all remaining ingredients to ensure they're gluten-free, as well.

INSTRUCTIONS:

1. Using a handheld or stand mixer, cream the butter, sugar, and extracts on medium speed until fluffy, about 1 minute. Scrape the sides and bottom of the bowl as needed.

2. In a separate bowl, whisk together the flour, cornstarch, and salt. Add the flour mixture to the wet ingredients and mix on low speed until all the flour is incorporated. The dough will be very thick and dry. Finish mixing by hand, if needed.

3. Divide the dough into 16 equal portions and roll each one into a ball. Place them on a parchment-lined or ungreased baking sheet about 2 inches (5 cm) apart. Carefully and slowly use the back of a round teaspoon or your thumb to press down and create an indentation on the top of each cookie ball. Mend any large cracks that occur in the process. (Small ones are fine!)

4. Place your sheet of raw cookies in the freezer for 30–45 minutes to firm up. When you're 15 minutes out, preheat your oven to 350°F (approx. 177 °C).

5. Once your oven is nice and piping hot, remove the baking sheet from the freezer and add one cherry from the cherry pie filling to the top of each cookie to fill the indentation.

6. Bake the cookies for 11–12 minutes or just until set; you do not want them to brown. To check for doneness, lightly touch the sides of the cookies with the very tip of a finger or the back side of a measuring spoon. If it doesn't leave an indentation, the cookies are done. (Do this with caution, of course! The cookies will be very hot.)

7. Allow the cookies to cool on the baking sheet. Once they're mostly cool, warm the white chocolate in the microwave in 30-second increments (stirring in between) or in a double boiler over medium heat just until melted. Do not let the chocolate get too hot, as it may curdle.

8. Transfer the white chocolate to a piping bag, or transfer to a resealable plastic bag and snip off just the tip of one corner to create a very small opening. Use the piping bag to drizzle the white chocolate across the tops of the cookies in a zigzag motion. For best results, practice zigzagging on parchment paper before applying the chocolate to the cookies.

STORAGE:
These cookies are flexible and can be stored in either airtight or non-airtight containers, tins, or on plates covered in foil or plastic wrap. It's best to keep them away from heat.

CUTOUT SUGAR COOKIES

Sugar cookies are often thought of as "the ultimate Christmas cookie" thanks to their holiday-themed shapes, colored frostings, sprinkles, and of course their simple and sweet flavor that everyone loves. This recipe is so much fun to make on your own or as a family Christmas activity.

YIELD: **15–17 COOKIES, DEPENDING ON COOKIE CUTTER SIZE**

INGREDIENTS:
- ½ c. (113 g) vegan butter or margarine, softened
- ½ c. + 2 Tbsp. (145 g) granulated sugar
- 2 tsp. vanilla extract
- 1 tsp. water
- 1 ⅓ c. (187 g) all-purpose flour
- ¼ tsp. baking soda
- Royal Icing (recipe follows)

FOR BEST GLUTEN-FREE VERSION:
Try using your favorite gluten-free all-purpose flour in place of the regular all-purpose flour. Check the labels for all remaining ingredients to ensure they're gluten-free, as well.

STORAGE:
Once the icing is completely dry, the cookies are best stored in airtight containers or on plates covered in plastic wrap to help keep them soft. This may vary depending on the thickness of the cookies.

INSTRUCTIONS:
1. Preheat your oven to 350°F (approx. 177°C).
2. With a handheld or stand mixer, cream together the butter, sugar, vanilla, and water until fluffy, about 1 minute.
3. In a separate bowl, stir together the flour and baking soda..
4. Add the flour mixture to the wet ingredients and mix on low speed until all the flour is incorporated. Scrape the sides and bottom of the bowl as needed.
5. Gather the dough into one ball in the mixing bowl and transfer to a well-floured flat surface. Note: If the dough is too crumbly to come together, mix in an extra 1 teaspoon of water and try again.
6. Roll out the dough using a rolling pin also coated in flour. For softer cookies, roll the dough out to ¼–½ inch (about .5cm – 1cm) thick. For crunchier cookies, aim for about ⅛ inch (.3 cm) thick. Cut out the cookies using your favorite cookie cutters, then use a thin spatula to transfer them to a parchment-lined or ungreased baking sheet. Gather the remaining dough, roll out again, and repeat the process until all the dough is used up. Note: If the dough is too sticky to work with, form it into two discs, wrap them in plastic wrap, and refrigerate for 30 minutes. When ready to roll out the cookies, remove the dough from the fridge and leave it out on the counter for a couple of minutes until it's soft enough to handle.
7. Bake the cookies in your preheated oven for 7–10 minutes. It's better to slightly underbake rather than overbake, so remove the cookies from the oven before the edges begin to brown.
8. Allow the cookies to cool on the baking sheet for at least 2 minutes before transferring to a cooling rack. Cool completely before making and applying the Royal Icing.

NOTES:
- While cutting cookie shapes, keep in mind that although flour from the cutting board won't show up on the baked cookies, any cracks or fingerprints made in the raw dough will appear on the baked cookies.
- The dough can be made up to a week ahead and chilled for later use; just be sure to wrap it in plastic wrap before chilling, then let it sit at room temperature for 10 minutes before using.

ROYAL ICING

For beautifully decorated cookies, a reliable royal icing that's easy to work with is key. This icing recipe never lets me down, and has helped our family create cookies we're proud to show off and share with others.

YIELD: ABOUT 1 ½ CUPS OF ICING

INGREDIENTS:
- ¼ c. (60 ml) aquafaba (the liquid inside a can of chickpeas / garbanzo beans)
- ¼ tsp. cream of tartar
- 1 ½ c. (195 g) powdered sugar (confectioners' sugar), measured then sifted, + more as needed
- 1 Tbsp. (15 ml) light corn syrup
- 1 tsp. vanilla extract
- ¼ tsp. almond extract
- Food coloring (optional)

FOR BEST GLUTEN-FREE VERSION:
The recipe should be gluten-free as is, but double-check ingredient labels to be sure.

INSTRUCTIONS:

1. Using a handheld or stand mixer with a whisk attachment, mix the aquafaba and cream of tartar on the highest speed possible until fluffy, bright white, and very thick, 5–7 minutes.

2. Add ¾ c. (98 g) of the powdered sugar and mix on medium speed until glossy, 30 seconds to 1 minute.

3. Add the remaining ¾ c. (98 g) powdered sugar, the corn syrup, vanilla extract, and almond extract and mix until incorporated.

4. Decide if your icing is thick enough by adding a small amount of icing to a piping bag fitted with a decorating tip (alternatively, you can decorate your cookies with a butter knife.) Test the icing on parchment paper or on one of your cookies to see if it runs. If it does, add up to ½ c. more powdered sugar a little at a time until the icing reaches a thick enough consistency.

5. Add the food coloring, if using, one drop at a time until you reach the desired color. If using multiple colors, divide the icing into small bowls and color each one separately.

6. Decorate cookies with icing, followed by sprinkles or other decorative candies, if you like. Allow iced cookies to set at room temperature until completely dry, 1–2 hours.

NOTES:
- Be sure to sift powdered sugar before adding to the mixing bowl.
- The more food coloring you add, the longer the icing may take to dry.
- For more precise decorating, use piping bags fitted with decorating tips.

SNICKERDOODLES

Your home will smell like Christmas as you bake these simple yet astounding snickerdoodle cookies. There's just something about these buttery soft cookies coated with cinnamon and sugar goodness that instantly makes you want to take a seat as you enjoy each and every bite.

YIELD: 18–21 COOKIES

INGREDIENTS:
Cookies:
- 1 ⅓ c. (187 g) all-purpose flour
- ¾ tsp. cream of tartar
- ¼ tsp. baking soda
- ¼ tsp. salt
- ½ c. (113 g) vegan butter or margarine, softened
- ¾ c. (173 g) granulated sugar
- 1 Tbsp. (15 ml) non-dairy milk
- 1 tsp. vanilla extract

Cinnamon-Sugar for Rolling:
- 2 Tbsp. (29 g) granulated sugar
- ¾ tsp. cinnamon

FOR BEST GLUTEN-FREE VERSION:
Try your favorite gluten-free all-purpose flour in place of the regular all-purpose flour. Check the labels for all remaining ingredients to ensure they're gluten-free, as well.

INSTRUCTIONS:
1. Preheat your oven to 350° (approx. 177 °C).
2. In a bowl, stir together the flour, cream of tartar, baking soda, and salt.
3. In a separate bowl, using a handheld or stand mixer, cream the butter and sugar on medium speed until fluffy, about 1 minute. Add the milk and vanilla extract and mix again, about 30 seconds.
4. Add the dry ingredients to the wet ingredients and mix on low until the dough comes together. Scrape the sides and bottom of the bowl as needed.
5. In a small bowl, combine the cinnamon and sugar for rolling.
6. Form 1 ½-inch (4-cm) dough balls and drop each one into the cinnamon-sugar mixture. Roll around to evenly coat, then place on a parchment-lined or ungreased baking sheet 2 inches (5 cm) apart from one another.
7. Once all the dough has been used, return each ball to the bowl containing the cinnamon-sugar and coat for a second time.
8. Place each dough ball back on the baking sheet and flatten with the palm of your hand ever so slightly.
9. Bake in your preheated oven for 7–9 minutes or just until set. Allow to cool on the baking sheet for 2 minutes before transferring to a cooling rack.

STORAGE:
These cookies are best kept in an airtight container or on a plate covered in plastic wrap.

SOFT AND CHEWY GINGER SNAPS

Truly a family favorite! My uncle Johnny has made these many times and my dad says he catches himself craving them regularly. These ginger cookies are a wondrous treat to enjoy anytime, but especially during the holiday season thanks to their sparkling snow-like sugar coating and the blast of ginger-cinnamony sweetness you get with each bite. My husband, Jeff, and I both agree that these cookies go splendidly with a hot cup of coffee or tea, and their large size certainly adds to the fun, too!

YIELD: 16 LARGE COOKIES

INGREDIENTS:
- 1 Tbsp. (8 g) ground flaxseed
- 3 Tbsp. (45 ml) water
- 1 ½ c. (210 g) all-purpose flour
- 1 ¼ c. (135 g) oat flour
- 2 tsp. baking soda
- ½ tsp. salt
- 1 tsp. cinnamon
- 1 tsp. ginger
- ½ tsp. ground cloves
- 1 c. (216 g) packed brown sugar
- ¾ c. (170 g) vegan butter *or* margarine, softened
- ¼ c. (59 ml) molasses
- ¼ c. (58 g) granulated sugar for rolling

FOR BEST GLUTEN-FREE VERSION:
Try using your favorite gluten-free all-purpose flour in place of the regular all-purpose flour. Check the labels for all remaining ingredients to ensure they're gluten-free, as well.

INSTRUCTIONS:
1. Preheat your oven to 375°F (approx. 190°C)
2. Combine the ground flaxseed and water in a small bowl and set aside.
3. In a medium-sized bowl, combine the flours, baking soda, salt, cinnamon, ginger, and cloves and stir to combine. Set aside.
4. Using a stand or handheld mixer, cream the brown sugar, butter, and molasses until fluffy, about 1 minute. Then add the flaxseed mixture and mix again for another 30 seconds.
5. Add half of the dry ingredients to the sugar mixture and mix on low until mostly combined. Then add the second half of the dry ingredients and mix again, this time starting on a low speed and then increasing to high as the dough becomes thick and hard to mix. Scrape the sides and bottom of the bowl as needed. The dough will be very thick when it's done.
6. Pour the granulated sugar into a bowl and set aside. Then form 16 golf ball–sized dough balls and place them on parchment-lined or ungreased baking sheets. Roll each ball in the granulated sugar to evenly coat, then return to the baking sheet, ensuring they're at least 3 inches (about 8 cm) apart from one another, as they will spread.
7. Bake the cookies one sheet at a time on the top rack in your preheated oven for 9–10 minutes or until cracks form across the surface. It's better to slightly underbake than to overbake. Allow the cookies to cool on the baking sheets for 3–5 minutes before transferring to a cooling rack.

STORAGE:
These cookies are flexible and can be stored in airtight or non-airtight containers, tins, or on plates covered in foil or plastic wrap.

PEPPERMINT CHOCOLATE CHUNK BROWNIE COOKIES

These peppermint chocolate chunk brownie cookies are like a soft, warm blanket of chocolatey, candy cane–brownie cookie goodness. They are loaded with rich chocolate chunks but also offer a perfect amount of fresh, crunchy peppermint and a hint of salt.

YIELD: 12–14 COOKIES

INGREDIENTS:
- 1 Tbsp. (8 g) finely ground flaxseed
- 3 Tbsp. (45 ml) water
- ⅔ c. (93 g) all-purpose flour
- ¼ c. (27 g) oat flour
- ½ c. (115 g) granulated sugar
- ¼ c. (54 g) packed brown sugar
- ¼ c. (20 g) cocoa powder
- ½ tsp. baking powder
- ¼ tsp. baking soda
- ½ tsp. salt
- ⅓ c. + 1 Tbsp. (94 ml) oil
- ¾ tsp. peppermint extract
- 1 c. (about 150 g) dairy-free chocolate chunks, chips, or chopped chocolate bar
- 3 Tbsp. (28 g) peppermint candy cane pieces (about 2 standard-sized candy canes, chopped)

FOR BEST GLUTEN-FREE VERSION:
For the best gluten-free version of this cookie, mix up one Peanut's Bake Shop® Midnight Chocolate Chunk Cookie Kit according to package directions and then add ¾ tsp. peppermint extract to the dough. Proceed with the instructions 5-7 above. Alternatively, you can try replacing the regular all-purpose flour called for in the recipe above with gluten-free all-purpose flour.

INSTRUCTIONS:
1. Preheat your oven to 350°F (approx. 177°C).
2. Combine the flaxseed and water in a small bowl and set aside.
3. In a mixing bowl, whisk together the flours, sugars, cocoa powder, baking powder, baking soda, and salt, breaking up the sugar and flour clumps along the way.
4. Add the oil, peppermint extract, the flaxseed mixture, and the chocolate chunks and stir until all the flour is incorporated. The dough will be very thick.
5. Divide the cookie dough into 12–14 equal-sized balls and place them on parchment-lined or ungreased baking sheets 3 inches (about 8 cm) apart from one another. Bake in your preheated oven for 12–13 minutes or until the surface of the cookies is matte rather than shiny. It's better to slightly underbake than to overbake.
6. Immediately upon removing them from the oven, with the cookies still on the baking sheets, top each cookie with a generous pinch of the candy cane pieces and lightly press down so they stick to the cookies' surfaces.
7. Transfer the candy cane–topped cookies to a cooling rack.

STORAGE:
Do not store these in airtight plastic storage containers or bags, otherwise the cookies may become overly chewy and the candy cane pieces will lose their crunch. Cardboard cookie boxes, metal cookie tins, or plates loosely covered in plastic wrap or foil work best.

GINGERBREAD FOLKS

When it comes to classic Christmas cookies, gingerbread people are always at the top of the list. My twin boys, Jack and James, absolutely adore them, especially if they're decorated with cute smiling faces and red cinnamon candies for buttons. In fact, I'm pretty sure that's why my two grown older brothers, Nick and Tim, love them so much, too!

YIELD: ABOUT 20 GINGERBREAD PEOPLE

INGREDIENTS:
- ¾ c. (162 g) packed brown sugar
- ½ c. (113 g) cold vegan butter or margarine
- ⅓ c. (79 ml) molasses
- 3 Tbsp. (45 ml) water
- 2 ⅔ c. (373 g) all-purpose flour
- ½ tsp. baking soda
- ½ tsp. salt
- ¾ tsp. ginger
- ¾ tsp. cinnamon
- ¼ tsp. nutmeg
- ¼ tsp. allspice
- Red cinnamon candies, sprinkles, or Royal Icing (page 24) for decor

FOR BEST GLUTEN-FREE VERSION:
Try using your favorite gluten-free all-purpose flour in place of the regular all-purpose flour. Check the labels for all remaining ingredients to ensure they're gluten-free, as well.

STORAGE:
These cookies are flexible and can be stored in airtight or non-airtight containers, tins, or on plates covered in foil or plastic wrap.

INSTRUCTIONS:
1. Preheat your oven to 350°F (approx. 177°C).
2. Using a handheld or stand mixer, cream the brown sugar, butter, and molasses on medium speed until the mixture is light brown and fluffy, about 1 minute. Scrape the sides and bottom of the bowl as needed. Add the water and mix again, about 10 seconds.
3. In a medium bowl, combine the flour, baking soda, salt, and all the spices. Add the dry ingredients to the butter mixture and mix until well combined. The dough will be very thick, so finish mixing by hand if needed.
4. Divide the dough in half and shape into two discs.
5. Transfer one disc to a floured work surface, and add a dusting of flour to both sides of the dough disc as well. Roll out the dough with a rolling pin, flouring the pin if it sticks, to about ¼ inch (about .6 cm) thick.
6. Use a gingerbread-person cookie cutter to create as many cookies as you can and transfer them to parchment-lined or ungreased baking sheets using a thin spatula.
7. Gather the leftover pieces of dough, shape into a new disc, and repeat the process. Keep in mind that any cracks or fingerprints will show up in the baked cookies, so keep them as smooth as possible. If using red cinnamon candies or other sprinkles to decorate, add them to the cookies before they are baked. Press down lightly to secure them into place on the dough.
8. Repeat steps 5–7 with your second disc of dough.
9. Bake the cookies for 7–8 minutes for a soft texture, or 9–10 minutes for crunchier cookies. Remove from the oven and immediately transfer the cookies to a cooling rack. Cool completely before decorating with Royal Icing.

NOTES:
- If the dough is too sticky to work with, wrap the dough discs in plastic and refrigerate for 20–30 minutes.
- While cutting cookie shapes, keep in mind that although flour from the cutting board won't show up on the baked cookies, any cracks or fingerprints made in the raw cookies will appear on the baked cookies.

OATMEAL RAISIN COOKIES

My grandma Norma is the oatmeal cookie baking queen. Throughout most of my childhood, there was hardly an occasion we'd walk into my grandparents' house and not instantly be taken with the comforting aroma of oatmeal cookies cooling on the kitchen counter. She'd swap out the mix-ins, though . . . sometimes she'd add nuts; other times butterscotch or chocolate chips. But the classic combo of oatmeal cookies with raisins was always my favorite. I created the recipe below in hopes of bringing the comforting feeling of "grandma's house" to your home, as well.

YIELD: 12 COOKIES

INGREDIENTS:

- 1 Tbsp. (8 g) ground flaxseed
- 3 Tbsp. (45 ml) water
- ½ c. (115 g) granulated sugar
- ⅓ c. + 2 Tbsp. (95 g) packed brown sugar
- ¼ c. + 2 Tbsp. (85 g) vegan butter or margarine, softened
- 1 tsp. vanilla extract
- 1 c. + 3 Tbsp. (166 g) all-purpose flour
- ½ tsp. baking soda
- ¼ tsp. salt
- 1 tsp. cinnamon
- ¼ tsp. nutmeg
- ¾ c. + 1 Tbsp. (110 g) rolled old-fashioned oats
- ⅔ c. (90 g) raisins

FOR BEST GLUTEN-FREE VERSION:
For the *very best* gluten-free oatmeal raisin cookies, use one Peanut's Bake Shop® Cinnamon Oatmeal Cookie Kit and add ⅓ c. (45 g) raisins to the dough before baking.

INSTRUCTIONS:

1. Preheat your oven to 350°F (approx. 177°C). Combine the ground flaxseed and water in a small bowl and set aside.

2. Using a handheld or stand mixer, cream the sugars, butter, and vanilla until fluffy, about 1 minute.

3. In a separate bowl, combine the flour, baking soda, salt, cinnamon, and nutmeg and stir.

4. Add the flour mixture and the ground flaxseed mixture to the butter mixture. Mix on medium-low speed until all the flour is incorporated. Scrape the sides and bottom of the bowl as needed.

5. Add the oats and raisins to the bowl and mix on low until evenly distributed.

6. Using your hands, form the dough into one big ball. If it is too dry to create a ball, mix in 1 teaspoon of water and try again.

7. Divide the dough into 12 equal-sized balls and place on a parchment-lined or ungreased baking sheet. Flatten dough balls ever so slightly with the palm of your hand. Be sure to space them 2–3 inches (about 5–8 cm) apart from one another as the cookies will spread. Use two baking sheets if necessary.

8. Bake the cookies in your preheated oven for 10–11 minutes or just until the tops of the cookies are set and matte rather than shiny. It's better to underbake than to overbake. Allow the cookies to cool for 2–3 minutes on the baking sheet before transferring to a cooling rack.

STORAGE:
The cookies are best stored in an airtight container or on a plate covered in plastic wrap.

PEPPERMINT PINWHEELS

A dazzling and delightful cookie, the peppermint pinwheel offers the perfect combination of fresh peppermint and sweet vanilla. The decorative sugar on top adds an extra sparkle and a slight crunch as you enjoy this festive candy cane–inspired cookie.

YIELD: ABOUT 24 PINWHEELS

INGREDIENTS:
- 2 ⅔ c. (374 g) all-purpose flour
- ½ tsp. baking soda
- 1 c. (226 g) vegan butter or margarine, softened
- 1 ¼ c. (288 g) granulated sugar
- 2 tsp. vanilla extract
- 2 tsp. peppermint extract
- 2 tsp. water
- ¼ tsp. red food coloring + more as needed
- Coarse decorative sparkling sugar for topping

FOR BEST GLUTEN-FREE VERSION:
Try your favorite gluten-free all-purpose flour in place of the regular all-purpose flour. Check the labels for all remaining ingredients to ensure they're gluten-free, as well.

STORAGE:
These cookies are flexible and can be kept in airtight containers or non-airtight containers, tins, or on plates covered with foil or plastic wrap. Refrain from stacking to prevent the sugar from falling off.

INSTRUCTIONS:
1. Mix together the flour and baking soda and set aside.
2. In a mixing bowl using a handheld or stand mixer, beat the butter and sugar until creamy, about 1 minute.
3. Add the extracts and water and mix well.
4. Add the dry ingredients to the wet ingredients and mix until the dough comes together and all the flour is incorporated. Scrape the sides and bottom of the bowl as needed.
5. Divide the dough in half as evenly as possible. Remove one half of the dough (about 450 g) from the bowl, form into a disc, and wrap in plastic.
6. Add the red food coloring to the dough remaining in the bowl and mix well.
7. Form the red dough into a disc, wrap in plastic, and chill both discs in the fridge for 20–30 minutes.
8. Working one disc at a time, roll each disc out onto its own well-floured sheet of parchment paper to create two rectangles approximately 9 x 13 ½ inches (23 x 33 cm) in size. Carefully return the red rectangle to the refrigerator for another 10 minutes.
9. After chilling, quickly yet carefully flip the red rectangle on top of the white one, aiming to match up the edges the best you can. Trim the edges with a sharp knife as needed.
10. Turn the dough so one of the short sides is facing you and begin rolling the dough into a log. It's best to use the parchment as a tool, lifting as you go. Roll as tightly as possible, mending and patching the dough as needed along the way. Cover the log in plastic wrap and chill in the refrigerator for at least 1 hour.
11. Once chilled, preheat your oven to 350°F (approx. 177°C) and remove the dough log from the fridge. Using a sharp knife, slice into roughly ¼-inch (½-cm) cookies and place on parchment-lined or ungreased baking sheets. Bake for 8–10 minutes or just until cookies are set, but not browned. Immediately add a generous pinch of decorating sugar to the surface of each cookie, then transfer to a cooling rack.

CLASSIC CHOCOLATE CHIP COOKIES

Chocolate chip cookies . . . the cookie of all cookies, the favorite of all favorites, the timeless cookie that we love as kids and even more so as adults. Therefore, it goes without saying that this classic cookie should be baked and enjoyed at Christmastime. They somehow make the happiest season of all feel even happier!

YIELD: **15–16 COOKIES**

INGREDIENTS:
- 1 Tbsp. (8 g) ground flaxseed
- 3 Tbsp. (45 ml) water
- ½ c. (113 g) vegan butter or margarine, softened
- ½ c. + 2 Tbsp. (144 g) granulated sugar
- ¼ c. (108 g) packed brown sugar
- 1 tsp. vanilla extract
- 1 ½ c. (210 g) all-purpose flour
- ½ tsp. baking soda
- ½ tsp. baking powder
- ½ tsp. salt
- 1 ¼ c. (about 210 g) dairy-free chocolate chips, chocolate chunks, or chopped chocolate bar, divided

FOR BEST GLUTEN-FREE VERSION:
Try a Peanut's Bake Shop® Chocolate Chunk Cookie Kit for the *very best* gluten-free chocolate chunk cookies.

INSTRUCTIONS:
1. Preheat your oven to 350°F (approx. 177°C).
2. Combine the ground flaxseed and water in a small bowl and set aside.
3. Using a handheld or stand mixer, cream the butter and sugars until fluffy, about 1 minute. Add the vanilla and ground flaxseed mixture and mix again until well combined.
4. In a separate bowl, stir together the flour, baking soda, baking powder, and salt. Add these dry ingredients to the butter mixture and mix until all the flour is incorporated. Scrape the sides and bottom of the bowl as needed.
5. Add 1 c. (168 g) of chocolate chips or chunks and mix until just combined.
6. Create fifteen to sixteen 1 ½-inch (4-cm) dough balls and place on parchment-lined or ungreased baking sheet(s) 3 inches (7 cm) apart from one another.
7. Bake in your preheated oven for 12–13 minutes or until the surface of the cookies is matte rather than shiny. It's better to underbake than overbake. Note: They may look puffy as you take them out of the oven, but don't worry—they will flatten as they cool. As soon as the cookies come out of the oven, dot the tops with the remaining ¼ c. (42 g) chocolate chips or chunks wherever you see fit. You want the cookies to be loaded with chocolate!
8. Allow the cookies to cool on the baking sheet(s) for 2–3 minutes before transferring to a cooling rack.

NOTE:
If you love a sweet and salty treat, sprinkle each cookie with coarse or flake salt after dotting each one with extra chocolate.

STORAGE:
These cookies are best stored in airtight containers or on plates covered in plastic wrap.

SPARKLING CITRUS GUMDROP COOKIES

These colorful cookies offer just the right amount of bright lemony sweetness that amazingly complements the individual flavors of each gumdrop. This simple recipe is a blast to make with the younger bakers in your life; just be sure to have extra gumdrops on hand, as they somehow manage to disappear during the cookie-making process.

YIELD: 20–21 COOKIES

INGREDIENTS:
- ¾ c. (170 g) vegan butter or margarine, softened
- ¾ c. (173 g) granulated sugar
- 2 Tbsp. (30 ml) non-dairy milk
- 2 ½ tsp. loosely packed lemon zest (from about 1 medium-sized lemon)
- ½ tsp. vanilla extract
- 2 ⅓ c. (244 g) all-purpose flour
- ¼ tsp. baking powder
- ¼ tsp. salt

For Decorating:
- ⅔ c. (about 133 g) vegan gum drops or gummy dot candies, sliced widthwise into 3 discs each
- 2–3 Tbsp. (29–43 g) sparkling decorating sugar or regular granulated sugar

FOR BEST GLUTEN-FREE VERSION:
Try your favorite gluten-free all-purpose flour in place of the regular all-purpose flour. Check the labels for all remaining ingredients to ensure they're gluten-free, as well.

STORAGE:
These cookies are flexible and can be kept in airtight or non-airtight containers, tins, or on plates covered with foil or plastic wrap.

INSTRUCTIONS:
1. Using a handheld or stand mixer, cream together the butter and sugar until fluffy, about 1 minute. Add the milk, lemon zest, and vanilla extract and mix again, about 30 seconds.
2. In a separate bowl, stir together the flour, baking soda, and salt. Add these dry ingredients to the bowl containing the butter mixture and mix on low until all the flour is incorporated. Scrape the sides and bottom of the bowl as needed.
3. Gather the dough into a ball, then divide it into 2 equal-sized discs. Wrap each in plastic wrap and refrigerate for 30–45 minutes. After the dough has chilled, preheat your oven to 350°F (approx. 177°C).
4. Remove the discs of dough from the fridge and place one of them on a floured surface. Roll the dough out to ¼ inch (about ½ cm) thick, dusting the rolling pin and surface of the dough with flour if needed.
5. Use a round cookie cutter 2–2 ½ inches (5–6.5 cm) in diameter to create dough circles, then use a thin spatula to carefully transfer them to a parchment-lined or ungreased baking sheet.
6. Gather and re-roll the dough scraps and cut more circles until all the dough is used up.
7. Decorate the tops of the cookies with gumdrop slices, lightly pressing as you go to help secure them. Use a toothpick to assist if they are sticky.
8. Bake in your preheated oven for 9–11 minutes or just until the cookies are set but not brown.
9. Immediately upon removing them from the oven, generously sprinkle the surface of each cookie with decorating or granulated sugar. Allow cookies to cool on the baking sheets for 3–5 minutes before transferring to a cooling rack.

NOTE:
Keep in mind that although flour from the cutting board won't show up on the baked cookies, any cracks or fingerprints in the raw dough will appear in the baked cookies.

PECAN SNOWDROPS

Also known as Mexican Wedding Cakes, Russian Tea Cakes, or Snowballs (just to name a few), these sugar-dusted cookies are loved all over the globe—including in the Dunham residence! My mom has been making these cookies every Christmas for as long as I can remember, mainly because they are my dad's absolute favorite. It's one cookie that we can always count on when receiving a Christmas cookie tin from my parents.

YIELD: **ABOUT 22 SNOWDROPS**

INGREDIENTS:
- ½ c. (113 g) vegan butter or margarine, softened
- ½ c. + 1 Tbsp. (73 g) powdered sugar (confectioners' sugar), divided
- ¾ tsp. vanilla extract
- 1 c. + 2 Tbsp. (158 g) all-purpose flour
- ⅓ c. + 1 Tbsp. (48 g) pecans, finely chopped*

*Chopped hazelnuts, almonds, or walnuts can be used in place of the pecans.

FOR BEST GLUTEN-FREE VERSION:
Try your favorite gluten-free all-purpose flour in place of the regular all-purpose flour. Check the labels for all remaining ingredients to ensure they're gluten-free, as well.

INSTRUCTIONS:

1. Preheat your oven to 400°F (approx. 200°C).

2. Using a handheld or stand mixer, cream the butter, ¼ c. (33 g) of the powdered sugar, and the vanilla extract until fluffy, about 1 minute.

3. Add the flour and pecans and mix on low until the dough holds together. Scrape the sides and bottom of the bowl as needed.

4. Shape the dough into 1-inch (3-cm) balls and place on parchment-lined or ungreased baking sheets 2 inches (5 cm) apart from one another.

5. Bake for 9–10 minutes or until the bottoms of the cookies are a deep medium brown. Keep cookies on baking sheets until just cool enough to handle.

6. Meanwhile, place the remaining ⅓ c. (43 g) powdered sugar in a bowl. While the cookies are still warm, roll each one in the powdered sugar and then set on a cooling rack.

7. Once the cookies are completely cool, roll in powdered sugar a second time.

NOTE:
For better coating, choose a powdered sugar that contains cornstarch in the ingredients.

STORAGE:
These snowdrops are flexible and can be stored in airtight or non-airtight containers, tins, or on plates covered with foil. Refrain from covering in plastic wrap as it may stick to the powdered sugar.

RED VELVET CRINKLE COOKIES

These dreamy red velvet crinkle cookies are like a Christmas present in cookie form. Soft and chewy red velvet cookies peeking through the cracks in their sweet, white powdery coating . . . it's no wonder these are my husband's favorite holiday cookies.

YIELD: 19–20 COOKIES

INGREDIENTS:

- 1 Tbsp. (8 g) ground flaxseed
- 3 Tbsp. (45 ml) water
- 1 ½ c. + 1 Tbsp. (219 g) all-purpose flour
- ¾ c. (81 g) oat flour
- ⅓ c. (27 g) cocoa powder
- 1 ½ tsp. baking powder
- ½ tsp. baking soda
- ½ tsp. salt
- ¾ c. (170 g) vegan butter or margarine, softened
- ¾ c. (162 g) packed brown sugar
- ½ c. (115 g) granulated sugar
- 2 tsp. vanilla extract
- ¾ tsp. red food coloring + more as needed

For Rolling:

- ½ c. (115 g) granulated sugar
- ½ c. (65 g) powdered sugar (confectioners' sugar)
- 2 tsp. (4 g) cornstarch

FOR BEST GLUTEN-FREE VERSION:

Try your favorite gluten-free all-purpose flour in place of the regular all-purpose flour. Check the labels for all remaining ingredients to ensure they're gluten-free, as well.

INSTRUCTIONS:

1. Combine the ground flaxseed and water in a small bowl and set aside.

2. In a medium bowl, stir together the flours, cocoa powder, baking powder, baking soda, and salt and set aside.

3. Using a handheld or stand mixer, cream the butter and sugars until fluffy, about 1 minute. Add the vanilla, food coloring, and the flaxseed mixture and mix until well combined, about 30 seconds. Scrape the sides and bottom of the bowl as needed.

4. Add half of the flour mixture to the wet ingredients and mix until the flour is incorporated. At this point, if you need more red color in your dough, add more food coloring ¼ tsp. at a time and mix until you've reached your desired red color. Add the second half of the flour mixture and mix again until all the flour is incorporated. Scrape the sides and bottom of the bowl again.

5. If the dough is too soft to form into balls, place the bowl of dough in the fridge for just 10 minutes to chill. If you can form balls, disregard this step. Preheat the oven to 325°F (approx. 163°C).

6. Place the granulated sugar in one small bowl and combine the powdered sugar and cornstarch in a separate small bowl.

7. Roll 1 ½ Tbsp. (30 g) of dough into a ball, drop it into the bowl of granulated sugar, and roll to evenly coat.

8. Place the dough ball on a parchment-lined or ungreased baking sheet. Repeat this process with the remaining dough.

9. Working one ball at a time, roll each granulated sugar–coated ball in the powdered sugar mixture, ensuring they are each *generously* coated and completely white. Place the balls back on the baking sheet, spacing them 2–3 inches (5–8 cm) apart.

10. Bake the cookies one baking sheet at a time on the top rack of the oven for 9–10 minutes, or until big cracks form across the tops of the cookies. Allow the cookies to cool for 10 minutes on the baking sheets before transferring to a cooling rack.

STORAGE:

Store the cookies away from heat in non-airtight tins or boxes, or on a foil-covered plate. Avoid airtight containers or covering in plastic wrap, as they may cause the powdered sugar to become sticky.

CLASSIC PEANUT BUTTER COOKIES

I know Santa loves the beautifully decorated sugar cookies and gingerbread folks, but word on the street is that he loves a plate of classic peanut butter cookies, too, especially when paired with a cold glass of almond or oat milk. Try making these for Santa this year so you can see for yourself—I'm betting you'll be left with hardly a crumb!

YIELD: 18–19 COOKIES

INGREDIENTS:
- 1 Tbsp. (8 g) ground flaxseed
- 3 Tbsp. (45 ml) water
- 1 ⅓ c. (187 g) all-purpose flour
- ½ tsp. baking powder
- ½ tsp. baking soda
- ½ tsp. cornstarch
- ½ tsp. salt
- ½ c. (113 g) vegan butter or margarine, softened
- ½ c. (115 g) granulated sugar
- ½ c. (108 g) packed brown sugar
- ½ c. (128 g) all-natural peanut butter, smooth or crunchy
- 1 tsp. vanilla extract

FOR BEST GLUTEN-FREE VERSION:
Try using your favorite gluten-free all-purpose flour in place of the regular all-purpose flour. Check the labels for all remaining ingredients to ensure they're gluten-free, as well.

INSTRUCTIONS:
1. Preheat your oven to 350°F (approx. 177°C).
2. In a small bowl, combine the ground flaxseed and water and set aside.
3. In a medium bowl, combine the flour, baking powder, baking soda, cornstarch, and salt and set aside.
4. Using a handheld or stand mixer, cream the butter and sugars until fluffy, about 1 minute.
5. Add the ground flaxseed mixture, peanut butter, and vanilla and mix again, about 30 seconds.
6. Finally, add the flour mixture to the bowl and mix until all dry ingredients are incorporated. Scrape down the sides and bottom of the bowl as needed.
7. Roll eighteen to nineteen 1 ½-inch (4-cm) dough balls and place on parchment-lined or ungreased baking sheets at least 3 inches (7 cm) apart from one another.
8. Using a fork, create the traditional crisscross marks on the top of each dough ball, pressing down ever so slightly. Mend any large cracks that occur around the edges (small cracks are fine!).
9. Bake the cookies in your preheated oven for 11–12 minutes or just until the tops are set and the surface is matte rather than shiny.
10. Allow them to cool for 5 minutes on the baking sheets before transferring to a cooling rack.

NOTE:
Be sure to use all-natural peanut butter that does not contain palm oil or coconut oil, as this will affect the texture of your dough.

STORAGE:
These cookies are flexible and can be stored in airtight or non-airtight containers, tins, or on plates covered in foil or plastic wrap.

CHRISTMAS KITCHEN SINK COOKIES

As the name indicates, these cookies are loaded with a wide variety of delicious flavors and fun textures, ranging from sweet chocolate and sprinkles, to chewy coconut and oats, to crunchy nuts and crispy rice cereal . . . all with just a hint of cinnamon and salt. These cookies are like a Christmas party in your mouth!

YIELD: **11 LARGE COOKIES**

INGREDIENTS:

- 1 Tbsp. + 1 tsp. (11 g) ground flaxseed
- ¼ c. (60 ml) water
- ¾ c. (27 g) crispy rice cereal
- ½ c. (70 g) all-purpose flour
- ½ c. (80 g) chopped dairy-free chocolate bar, chopped into ¼-½ inch (about .5-1.5 cm) chunks
- ⅓ c. + 1 Tbsp. (91 g) granulated sugar
- ⅓ c. (33 g) old-fashioned rolled oats
- ⅓ c. (37 g) shredded coconut or (27 g) flaked coconut
- 3 Tbsp. (23 g) pecans or other nut of choice, chopped into pea-sized pieces
- 3 Tbsp. (35 g) dairy-free chocolate chips
- ½ tsp. salt
- ½ tsp. baking powder
- ¼ tsp. baking soda
- ¼ tsp. cinnamon
- ⅓ c. (79 ml) oil
- 1 tsp. vanilla extract
- 3 Tbsp. (36 g) red, white, and green sprinkles (1 Tbsp. of each color, if in separate bottles) + more for topping
- A couple pinches of coarse or flake salt (optional, but recommended)

FOR BEST GLUTEN-FREE VERSION:
Try using your favorite gluten-free all-purpose flour in place of the regular all-purpose flour. Check the labels for all remaining ingredients to ensure they're gluten-free, as well.

INSTRUCTIONS:

1. Preheat your oven to 350°F (approx. 177°C).
2. In a small bowl, combine the ground flaxseed and water and set aside.
3. In a medium-sized mixing bowl, combine the crispy rice cereal, flour, chopped chocolate, sugar, rolled oats, coconut, pecans, chocolate chips, salt, baking powder, baking soda, and cinnamon and stir well.
4. Add the oil, vanilla extract, and ground flaxseed mixture to the bowl and stir until all the flour is incorporated.
5. Fold in the sprinkles.
6. Form one tightly packed dough ball using either a ¼-c. / no. 16 (72g) scoop or a ¼ c. measuring cup. Place the scoop or measuring cup facedown on a parchment-lined or ungreased baking sheet and slowly release the dough ball. Reshape as needed on the baking sheet, doing the best you can to form a ball. Repeat this step ten more times with the remaining cookie dough.
7. Once all the dough balls are formed, add any chocolate chips or dough remaining in the bottom of the bowl to the tops of the dough balls.
8. Bake the cookies in your preheated oven for 13–14 minutes or until the tops are set and the edges of the cookies turn a light golden color. Add an extra pinch of sprinkles to the surface of each cookie as soon as they come out of the oven, then add a pinch of flake or coarse salt, if you like. Allow the cookies to cool for 3–5 minutes on the baking sheet(s) before transferring to a cooling rack.

NOTE:
This is a loose cookie dough, so pack your cup or scoop tightly before transferring the dough to your baking sheet.

STORAGE:
These cookies are best kept in an airtight container or on a plate covered in plastic wrap.

SPRITZ COOKIES

Beautifully detailed and buttery sweet, spritz cookies are such a joy to make and especially fun to eat! My boys, Jack and James, just love helping me pick the shapes we make with our cookie press. The little trees and snowflakes are always among their top choices at Christmastime.

YIELD: **55–60 SMALL COOKIES**

INGREDIENTS:
Cookies:
- ½ c. (113 g) vegan butter or margarine, softened
- ¾ c. (98 g) powdered sugar (confectioners' sugar)
- 1 tsp. vanilla extract or almond extract (or a combination of the two)
- 2 Tbsp. (30 ml) non-dairy milk
- 1 ¼ c. + 2 Tbsp. (193g) all-purpose flour
- ¼ tsp. baking soda
- ¼ tsp. salt

Glaze:
- 1 c. (130 g) powdered sugar (confectioners' sugar)
- 3 Tbsp. (23 ml) non-dairy milk
- ½ tsp. vanilla extract or almond extract (or combination of the two)

FOR BEST GLUTEN-FREE VERSION:
Try your favorite gluten-free all-purpose flour in place of the regular all-purpose flour. Check the labels for all remaining ingredients to ensure they're gluten-free, as well.

INSTRUCTIONS:
1. Preheat your oven to 350°F (approx. 177°C). Place 12 baking sheets in the freezer to chill.
2. Using a handheld or stand mixer, cream together the butter, sugar, and extracts of choice on medium speed until fluffy, about 1 minute. Add the milk and mix again until combined. Scrape the sides and bottom of the bowl as needed.
3. In a separate bowl, stir together the flour, baking soda, and salt. Add the dry ingredients to the bowl containing the butter mixture and mix on low until combined, then increase the speed to medium for about 20 seconds or until the dough appears very fluffy.
4. Fill a cookie press with dough and press out shapes onto your chilled, ungreased baking sheets about 2 inches (5 cm) apart according to your cookie press instructions. Note: Do not line your baking sheets with parchment paper or the cookies may not stick.
5. Bake the cookies in your preheated oven for 6–7 minutes or until they are set, but not browned. Allow the cookies to cool on the baking sheets for 3–5 minutes before transferring to a cooling rack.
6. Once the cookies are completely cool, stir all the glaze ingredients together in a bowl. Using a pastry brush, lightly apply glaze to the tops of the cookies, then return them to the cooling rack. Alternatively, you can dip the tops of the cookies in the glaze. Immediately top with colored sugar or other sprinkles, if you like. Allow them to set at room temperature until dry, about 30 minutes.

NOTES:
- A cookie press is needed for this recipe. In my experience, it's worth it to spend just a little more for a higher quality one, as you seem to get what you pay for in this case.
- The dough can be made up to a week ahead and chilled for later use; just be sure to wrap it in plastic wrap before chilling, and bring it to room temperature before using it in your cookie press.

STORAGE:
These cookies are flexible and can be stored in airtight or non-airtight containers, tins, or on plates covered with foil or plastic wrap.

CRANBERRY ORANGE COCONUT CHEWIES

These unique cookies offer a glorious buttery, coconut, and orange aroma. They are chewy yet light, with the subtle flavor of orange and bits of tangy sweet cranberries. These chewies truly add a nice variety of flavors, textures, and colors to your holiday cookie platters.

YIELD: 15–16 COOKIES

INGREDIENTS:

- ½ c. (113 g) vegan butter or margarine, softened
- ¾ c. (173 g) granulated sugar
- 1 Tbsp. lightly packed orange zest (from approx. 1 large orange)
- ½ tsp. vanilla extract
- ⅔ c. (72 g) oat flour
- ⅓ c. + 2 Tbsp. (61 g) all-purpose flour
- ½ tsp. baking soda
- ¼ tsp. salt
- ¾ c. shredded coconut (80 g) *or* flaked coconut (60 g)
- ⅔ c. (86 g) dried cranberries

FOR BEST GLUTEN-FREE VERSION:
Use garbanzo bean (chickpea) flour (65 g) in place of the all-purpose flour. Check the labels for all remaining ingredients to ensure they're gluten-free, as well.

INSTRUCTIONS:

1. Preheat your oven to 350°F (approx. 177°C).
2. With a stand or handheld mixer, cream the butter, sugar, and orange zest on medium speed until fluffy, about 1 minute.
3. Add the vanilla extract and mix again, about 30 seconds.
4. In a separate bowl, combine the oat flour, all-purpose flour, baking soda, and salt and stir well.
5. Add the dry ingredients to the bowl containing the butter mixture and mix on low speed until all the flour is incorporated. Scrape the sides and bottom of the bowl as needed.
6. Add the coconut and dried cranberries to the bowl and mix on low once again just until both are well distributed throughout the cookie dough.
7. Place 1½-inch (about 4-cm) dough balls on parchment-lined or ungreased baking sheets and then flatten them ever so slightly with the palm of your hand. Be sure to space them 2–3 inches (about 5-8 cm) apart from one another as the cookies will spread.
8. Bake in your preheated oven for 10–12 minutes or until the edges just start to turn a golden color. It's better to slightly underbake than to overbake.
9. Allow the cookies to cool on the baking sheets for 5 minutes before transferring to a cooling rack.

STORAGE:
The cookies are best kept in an airtight container or on a plate covered in plastic wrap.

LINZER COOKIES

Sweet raspberry jam, magically soft cookies and a generous dusting of powdered sugar all come together to create one of the most loved and heartwarming cookies of all time. Arrange them on a cake pedestal or platter, and watch as fingers of all sizes reach in to steal them away.

YIELD: 14–16 COOKIES

INGREDIENTS:
- 2 ¼ c. (315 g) all-purpose flour
- ½ tsp. salt
- ¼ tsp. baking powder
- ¾ c. (170 g) vegan butter or margarine, slightly softened
- ¾ c. (173 g) granulated sugar
- 2 Tbsp. (30 ml) non-dairy milk
- 2 tsp. vanilla extract
- ¼ tsp. almond extract (optional)
- 3 Tbsp. (24 g) powdered sugar (confectioners' sugar) + more as needed
- About ¼ c. + 2 Tbsp. (108 g) red jam, such as raspberry or strawberry (the brighter red the better, and seedless, if possible)

FOR BEST GLUTEN-FREE VERSION:
Try your favorite gluten-free all-purpose flour in place of the regular all-purpose flour. Check the labels for all remaining ingredients to ensure they're gluten-free, as well.

INSTRUCTIONS:
1. In a medium bowl, combine the flour, salt, and baking powder and stir well to mix. Set aside.
2. In a mixing bowl using a handheld or stand mixer, beat the butter and granulated sugar until creamy, about 1 minute. Add the milk, vanilla extract, and almond extract, if using, and mix well.
3. Add the flour mixture to the wet ingredients and mix until the dough comes together and all the flour is incorporated. Scrape the sides and bottom of the bowl as needed.
4. Gather the dough into a ball, then divide it into 2 equal-sized discs. Wrap each in plastic wrap and refrigerate for 30–45 minutes. After the dough has chilled, preheat your oven to 350°F (approx. 177°C).
5. Remove the discs of dough from the fridge and place one of them on a floured surface. Roll the dough out to ⅛–¼ inch (¼-½ cm) thick, depending on how tall you would like your sandwich cookies. If the dough sticks, flour the surface of the dough and the rolling pin, as well. Using a round, scalloped cookie cutter about 2 inches (5–6 cm) in diameter (or other cookie cutter of choice), cut shapes into the dough, then use a thin spatula to transfer the cookies to a parchment-lined or ungreased baking sheet 2 inches (5 cm) apart from one another. Gather and re-roll the remaining dough until it's all used up.
6. The second disc of dough will be used to make the top halves of the cookies. Roll the dough out and cut cookies using the same cutter as for the previous batch, then use mini cookie cutters to cut out hearts, stars, or other shapes from the center of each cookie. Place the top halves on a parchment-lined or ungreased baking sheet as well.
7. Bake in your preheated oven for 7–8 minutes or just until set. Do not let them brown.

Recipe continues

8. Cool on the baking sheets for 3–5 minutes before transferring to a cooling rack. While still warm, liberally dust the top halves of the cookies (with the mini cutouts) with a first coating of powdered sugar using a fine-mesh sieve or flour sifter. Once completely cooled, dust with a second coating.

9. Just before serving, decide whether the top halves need one more coating of powdered sugar and apply if necessary. Spoon 1–2 tsp. of jam onto each of the bottom-layer cookies and spread evenly to reach all edges of the circle. To assemble, place the powdered sugared top halves on top of the bottom halves so that the jam shows through the cutout.

NOTES:
• While cutting cookie shapes, keep in mind that although flour from the cutting board won't show up on the baked cookies, any cracks or fingerprints in the raw dough will appear on the baked cookies.

• If you're not enjoying the cookies right away, wait until the last minute to assemble them in case you need to add an extra dusting of powdered sugar.

STORAGE:
These cookies are flexible and can be stored in airtight or non-airtight containers, tins, or on plates covered with foil or plastic wrap.

BARS AND OTHER TREATS

CHOCOLATE CHIP FUDGE BROWNIES

Chocolate lovers, this one's for you! These decadent brownies are super moist and fudgy with the added fun texture of chocolate chips. Enjoy them on their own or as the base for brownie ice cream sundaes.

YIELD: 16 SQUARE BROWNIES

INGREDIENTS:

- 1 Tbsp. (8 g) ground flaxseed
- 2 Tbsp. (30 ml) water
- 1 ¼ c. (175 g) all-purpose flour
- 1 c. + 1 Tbsp. (244 g) granulated sugar
- ½ c. (40 g) cocoa powder
- 1 tsp. baking powder
- ¾ tsp. salt
- ½ c. (119 ml) oil + more for greasing*
- ⅓ c. (79 ml) non-dairy milk
- 1 Tbsp. (15 ml) vanilla extract
- ¾ c. + 3 Tbsp. (about 171 g) dairy-free mini or regular chocolate chips, divided

*Alternatively, cooking spray can be used for greasing.

FOR BEST GLUTEN-FREE VERSION:

Try using your favorite gluten-free all-purpose flour in place of the regular all-purpose flour. Check the labels for all remaining ingredients to ensure they're gluten-free, as well.

STORAGE:

These brownies are best stored on a plate covered in plastic wrap or in an airtight container. If not serving right away, store them in the refrigerator and remove 1–2 hours before serving. Leftovers can be kept at room temperature.

INSTRUCTIONS:

1. Preheat your oven to 350°F (approx. 177°C). Grease an 8-x-8-inch (20-x-20-cm) pan with cooking spray or oil. Measure a sheet of parchment paper approximately 16 ½ x 6 inches (42 x 15 cm) in size and lay it across the center of the greased pan. Press down so the paper sticks to the oil. In the end, you should have about 3 inches (8 cm) of paper overhang on two opposite ends of the pan; these will serve as handles to later lift the brownies out of the pan. Set the pan aside.

2. In a small bowl, combine the flaxseed and water and set aside.

3. In a mixing bowl, whisk together the flour, sugar, cocoa powder, baking powder, and salt.

4. Add the oil, milk, vanilla extract, and flaxseed mixture to the bowl and stir to combine. The batter will be very thick.

5. Gently fold in ⅔ c. (124 g) of the chocolate chips.

6. Transfer the brownie batter to the prepared pan and gently spread so that it reaches all sides and corners. Pat the surface lightly with your fingertips to help smooth it over.

7. Sprinkle the remaining ¼ c. (47 g) of chocolate chips evenly over the surface.

8. Bake the brownies in your preheated oven for 23–25 minutes, or until the surface is set and the edges have just started to puff up and pull away from the pan.

9. Place the pan on a cooling rack to cool. Note: The brownies will likely sink in the center as they cool. This is perfectly normal and is a sign that your brownies will be extra fudgy.

10. Once the brownies are cool, place the pan in the fridge for at least an hour or until you're ready for them. Then, while still cold, slide a thin knife along the two sides of the pan not covered in parchment paper. Using the parchment handles, lift the brownies out of the pan and set them on a cutting board. Cut into 16 squares.

NOTES:

Want to add nuts? Go for it; about ¼ c. (about 38 g) of chopped nuts added to the batter will do.

SALTED BUTTER RUM BLONDIES

With their sweet and slightly salted butter flavor and a hint of boozy rum, these ooey-gooey blondies are ideal for evening Christmas parties and gatherings. Just add a few lit candles and some holiday music to set the mood, and you're well on your way to having a memorable and delicious night.

YIELD: 16 SQUARE BLONDIES

INGREDIENTS:

- oil or cooking spray for greasing
- 2 Tbsp. (16 g) ground flaxseed
- ¼ c. + 2 Tbsp. (90 ml) water
- 2 c. + 2 Tbsp. (298 g) all-purpose flour
- 1 tsp. baking powder
- 1 tsp. salt
- ¼ tsp. nutmeg
- 1 ¾ c. (378 g) packed brown sugar
- ½ c. + 1 Tbsp. (127 g) vegan butter or margarine, melted
- 2 ½ Tbsp. (37 ml) dark rum
- 1 Tbsp. (15 ml) non-dairy milk
- 1 tsp. vanilla extract
- 1 c. (112 g) walnuts, chopped
- A few pinches of coarse or flake salt

FOR BEST GLUTEN-FREE VERSION:
Try using your favorite gluten-free all-purpose flour in place of the regular all-purpose flour. If your gluten-free flour doesn't already contain it, add ½ tsp. of xanthan gum, as well.

STORAGE:
These blondies are best stored on a plate covered in plastic wrap or in an airtight container. If not serving right away, store them in the refrigerator and remove 1–2 hours before serving. Leftovers can be kept at room temperature.

INSTRUCTIONS:

1. Preheat your oven to 350°F (approx. 177°C). Grease an 8-x-8-inch (20-x-20-cm) pan with cooking spray or oil. Measure a sheet of parchment paper approximately 16 ½ x 6 inches (42 x 15 cm) in size and lay it across the center of the greased pan. Press down so the paper sticks to the oil. In the end, you should have about 3 inches (8 cm) of paper overhang on two opposite ends of the pan; these will serve as handles to later lift the blondies out of the pan. Set the pan aside.

2. In a small bowl, combine the flaxseed and water and set aside.

3. In a medium bowl, combine the flour, baking powder, salt, and nutmeg and set aside.

4. In a mixing bowl, whisk together the brown sugar, melted butter, rum, milk, and vanilla extract, until most of the sugar clumps are broken up.

5. Add the flour mixture as well as the flaxseed mixture to the wet ingredients and stir just until the flour is incorporated. Be careful not to overmix.

6. Gently fold in the chopped nuts.

7. Pour this thick mixture into your prepared pan and smooth over the surface so the batter reaches all sides and corners. Use your fingertips to assist if needed.

8. Bake in your preheated oven for 26-27 minutes or until the edges have puffed up and the center is set. In addition, the surface should appear matte rather than shiny.

9. Immediately after removing from the oven, crumble and sprinkle a few pinches of coarse salt evenly over the surface of the blondies.

10. Place the pan on a cooling rack. Note: The blondies may sink in the center as they cool. This is perfectly normal and is a sign that your blondies will be extra moist and ooey-gooey.

11. Once the blondies are cool, place the pan in the fridge for at least an hour or until you're ready for them. Then, while still cold, slide a thin knife along the two sides of the pan not covered in parchment paper. Using the parchment handles, lift the blondies out of the pan and set them on a cutting board. Cut into 16 squares.

PECAN PIE BARS

These pecan pie bars offer buttery-sweet pecan deliciousness with a flavorful, flakey crust, just like traditional pecan pie. They are an insanely addictive treat that the whole family will love!

YIELD: **24 SQUARE BARS**

INGREDIENTS:
• oil or cooking spray for greasing

Crust:
• 1 c. (140 g) all-purpose flour
• ½ c. (57 g) almond flour
• ½ c. (115 g) granulated sugar
• ½ tsp. salt
• ½ c. (113 g) cold vegan butter or margarine

Filling:
• 1 (13.66-oz. / 403-ml) can full-fat coconut milk (shake well before opening)
• ¼ c. + 3 Tbsp. (56 g) cornstarch
• ¼ c. + 2 Tbsp. (85 g) vegan butter or margarine
• ¾ c. (177 ml) maple syrup
• ¾ c. (162 g) packed brown sugar
• 1 tsp. salt
• 2 ½ tsp. vanilla extract
• 1 ¾ c. (210 g) chopped pecans, divided

FOR BEST GLUTEN-FREE VERSION:
Try using your favorite gluten-free all-purpose flour in place of the regular all-purpose flour. Check the labels for all remaining ingredients to ensure they're gluten-free, as well.

INSTRUCTIONS:
1. Preheat your oven to 350°F (approx. 177°C). Lightly grease a 9-x-13-inch (23-x-33-cm) pan with oil or cooking spray and set it aside.

2. To prepare the crust layer, mix the flours, sugar, and salt together in a mixing bowl, then cut the butter in using a pastry cutter, fork, food processor, or your fingertips. The finished crust dough will be very dry and will not resemble pie crust dough—but that's ok!

3. Press the crust mixture into the bottom of the prepared pan, ensuring it reaches all corners and edges.

4. Prick the surface several times with a fork, then bake in your preheated oven for 14–15 minutes. The crust does not need to be brown.

5. While the crust bakes, prepare your filling. Start by mixing together the coconut milk and cornstarch in a bowl. Set aside.

6. In a saucepan over medium heat, combine the butter, maple syrup, brown sugar, and salt and stir until the butter is melted and the sugar is mostly dissolved.

7. Add the coconut milk mixture to the saucepan and whisk frequently just until the edges start to rapidly bubble and the mixture starts to thicken. Watch closely and *immediately* turn off the heat and remove the pan from the burner once it reaches this stage. Stir in the vanilla and 1 ¼ c. (150 g) of the chopped pecans. Pour the filling mixture over the crust and smooth over the surface. Sprinkle the remaining ½ c. (60 g) chopped pecans across the top.

8. Bake for 20–25 minutes or until very bubbly and there is very little jiggle in the middle. Cool completely on a cooling rack before cutting into 24 square bars.

STORAGE:
The pecan pie bars are flexible and can be stored in airtight or non-airtight containers, tins, or on plates covered in foil or plastic wrap.

DATE BARS

There's something extra special and comforting about date bars ... maybe it's the fact that many of us enjoyed them as kids, or maybe it's simply because they're loaded with dates and oatmeal and sweet goodness. Either way, you can never go wrong with making date bars; they're a timeless classic.

YIELD: 24 SQUARE BARS

INGREDIENTS:
• oil or cooking spray for greasing

Filling:
• 3 c. (1 lb. / 454 g) pitted and chopped dates
• 1 ⅓ c. (319 ml) water
• 3 Tbsp. (45 ml) maple syrup

Crumb Layers:
• 1 c. (226 g) vegan butter or margarine, softened
• ¾ c. (173 g) granulated sugar
• 1 ½ c. (168 g) rolled old-fashioned oats
• ¾ c. (105 g) all-purpose flour
• ¾ c. (81 g) oat flour
• ½ tsp. salt
• ½ tsp. baking soda
• ¼ tsp. cinnamon (optional)

FOR BEST GLUTEN-FREE VERSION:
Try using your favorite gluten-free all-purpose flour in place of the regular all-purpose flour. Check the labels for all remaining ingredients to ensure they're gluten-free, as well.

INSTRUCTIONS:
1. Preheat your oven to 400°F (approx. 200°C).
2. Grease a 9-x-13-inch (23-x-33cm) baking dish with oil or cooking spray and set aside.
3. Combine all the filling ingredients in a saucepan over medium heat and cook, stirring frequently, until it looks like jam, about 7–10 minutes.
4. Remove from the heat and set aside to cool for at least 5 minutes.
5. Meanwhile, in a large bowl, stir together the butter and sugar. Add the oats, all-purpose flour, oat flour, salt, baking soda, and cinnamon, if using, and stir well until crumbly. You may need to use your hands in order to incorporate all of the flour.
6. Add half of this crumb mixture to your prepared pan and press until it is flat and reaches all edges and corners.
7. Add the date mixture to the pan, carefully smoothing over the surface so it reaches all edges and corners as well.
8. Sprinkle the remaining crumb mixture evenly over the surface. It's okay if you can see a little of the date mixture here and there. Lightly press down with your hand or a flat spatula.
9. Bake in your preheated oven for 24–26 minutes or until bits of the surface start to turn golden brown.
10. Cool on a cooling rack. Once cool, cut into 24 square bars.

STORAGE:
These date bars are flexible and can be stored in airtight or non-airtight containers, tins, or on plates covered in foil or plastic wrap.

FRUITCAKE BARS

Many fruitcake recipes are long and involved, taking hours to properly prepare and bake. In fact, my mom usually sets an entire day aside to make our family's generations-old fruitcake recipe, knowing many of us are counting on receiving a loaf in our Christmas baskets. Thankfully, this fruitcake bar recipe is here as a delightful quick and easy alternative, offering those same flavors we all know and love, but with a soft and chewy cookie-like base, and made in a fraction of the time.

YIELD: 24 BARS

INGREDIENTS:
- 1 Tbsp. (8 g) ground flaxseed
- 3 Tbsp. (45 ml) water
- ½ c. (113 g) vegan butter or margarine, softened, + more for greasing pan
- 1 ⅓ c. (288 g) packed brown sugar
- 1 Tbsp. (15 ml) non-dairy milk
- 1 ½ c. (210 g) all-purpose flour
- ½ tsp. salt
- ½ tsp. baking soda
- ½ tsp. cinnamon
- ¼ tsp. ground cloves
- ¼ tsp. nutmeg
- 1 ½ c. (255 g) candied fruit, chopped*
- 1 c. (120 g) chopped pecans or 1 c. (112 g) chopped walnuts
- ½ c. (68 g) raisins

*When it comes to candied fruit, I prefer a blend of cherries, orange, lemon peel, pineapple, and/or apricot.

FOR BEST GLUTEN-FREE VERSION:
Try your favorite gluten-free all-purpose flour in place of the regular all-purpose flour. Check the labels for all remaining ingredients to ensure they're gluten-free, as well.

INSTRUCTIONS:
1. Preheat your oven to 350°F (approx. 177°C). Grease a 9-x-13-inch (22-x-33-cm) baking dish with vegan butter and set aside.
2. In a small bowl, combine the ground flaxseed and water and set aside.
3. Using a handheld or stand mixer, cream the butter and sugar until fluffy, about 1 minute. Add the milk and ground flaxseed mixture and mix again, about 30 seconds.
4. In a separate bowl, stir together the flour, salt, baking soda, cinnamon, cloves, and nutmeg. Add the dry ingredients to the bowl containing the butter mixture and mix on low until all the flour is incorporated. Scrape the sides and bottom of the bowl as needed.
5. Transfer the dough to the prepared baking dish and press until it is flat and reaches all sides and corners of the bottom of the pan.
6. Next, stir together the candied fruit, nuts, and raisins and sprinkle over the surface of the dough.
7. Bake in your preheated oven for 25 minutes. Place the dish on a cooling rack. These bars can be served warm or at room temperature, but wait at least 10 minutes before cutting into squares.

STORAGE:
These fruitcake bars are flexible and can be stored in airtight or non-airtight containers, tins, or on plates covered with foil or plastic wrap.

CHOCOLATE-DIPPED COCONUT MACAROONS

You won't believe how easy it is to achieve traditionally delicious coconut macaroons just by following this simple recipe. Dipping these macaroons in chocolate certainly takes them to another level, and helps to create a "snowballs in the mud" look, as my husband, Jeff, playfully calls it!

YIELD: **12 MACAROONS**

INGREDIENTS:

- 1 c. (106 g) shredded coconut (*not* flaked coconut)
- ¼ c. (58 g) granulated sugar
- 2 Tbsp. (18 g) all-purpose flour
- ¼ c. (59 ml) canned full-fat coconut milk (shake well before opening and stir contents before measuring)
- ½ tsp. vanilla extract
- ¼ tsp. salt
- ½ c. (93 g) dairy-free chocolate chips or chopped chocolate bar
- ½–1 tsp. coconut oil (if needed)

FOR BEST GLUTEN-FREE VERSION:

Try using your favorite gluten-free all-purpose flour in place of the regular all-purpose flour. Check the labels for all remaining ingredients to ensure they're gluten-free, as well.

INSTRUCTIONS:

1. Preheat your oven to 350°F (approx. 177°C).
2. In a mixing bowl, stir together the coconut, sugar, flour, coconut milk, vanilla, and salt until well combined.
3. Using a 1 Tbsp. / no. 60 (20g) retractable scoop, create 12 equal-sized coconut balls and drop each one onto a parchment-lined or ungreased baking sheet.
4. Bake in your preheated oven for 15–16 minutes or until the edges and some tips are golden brown. Allow the macaroons to cool on the baking sheets.
5. Once the macaroons are completely cool, melt the chocolate in 30-second increments (stirring in between) in the microwave, or in a double boiler over medium heat. If your chocolate is not velvety-smooth once melted, add the coconut oil a little at a time until desired consistency is reached.
6. Dip the bottom of each macaroon into the melted chocolate, twisting it gently in the chocolate to ensure it's thoroughly coated around the bottom rim. Return each coated macaroon to the baking sheet and let sit at room temperature for about 1 hour to set.

STORAGE:

These macaroons are best kept in airtight containers or on a plate covered with plastic wrap.

BUTTERSCOTCH HAYSTACKS

Introducing my all-time favorite Christmas treat: butterscotch haystacks! There's just something about the sweet and slightly salty combination of butterscotch and peanut butter that has made me a big fan of these treats for as long as I can remember. Add mini marshmallows and crunchy noodles to that mix and you have a crazy-delicious blend of flavors and textures that's hard to resist.

YIELD: 27–28 HAYSTACKS

INGREDIENTS:
- 1 ½ c. (134 g) vegan mini marshmallows
- 1 ⅓ c. (73 g) crunchy chow mein noodles
- 1 c. (172 g) vegan butterscotch chips
- ½ c. (128 g) peanut butter
- 2 Tbsp. (28 g) vegan butter or margarine
- ¼ tsp. salt

FOR BEST GLUTEN-FREE VERSION:
Use gluten-free chow mein noodles or gluten-free pretzel sticks chopped into 1-inch (about 2.5-cm) pieces to replace the regular chow mein noodles. Check the labels for all remaining ingredients to ensure they're gluten-free, as well.

INSTRUCTIONS:
1. In a large mixing bowl, stir together the marshmallows and chow mein noodles. Set aside.
2. In a double boiler over medium heat, combine the butterscotch chips, peanut butter, butter, and salt and heat, stirring frequently, until fully melted. Alternatively, you can heat them in a medium-sized, microwave-safe bowl in the microwave in 30-second intervals, stirring in between each interval, until just melted. Do not overheat.
3. Pour the butterscotch mixture over the noodle and marshmallow mix and stir well until all the marshmallows are coated.
4. Drop about 1 ½-Tbsp. portions of the mix onto a parchment-lined or ungreased baking sheet to create 27–28 stacks.
5. Allow to sit at room temperature for 1–2 hours, or until set. For faster setting, place in the refrigerator for 20 minutes.

NOTES:
- Add an extra layer of flavor by adding chopped nuts. Simply swap out ¼ c. (22 g) chow mein noodles for ¼ c. (about 38 g) of your nut of choice. I like chopped pistachios or slivered almonds.
- Can't find vegan butterscotch chips? Simply swap them out for dairy-free chocolate chips instead.
- Once completely set, place the haystacks in cupcake liners or other paper cups for an extra-special presentation.

STORAGE:
These haystacks are flexible and can be stored in airtight or non-airtight containers, tins, or on plates covered with foil or plastic wrap.

CEREAL TREAT WREATHS

Nothing brings jolly to a holiday cookie platter like these adorable cereal treat wreaths! With their green holly leaves, bright red cinnamon berries, fun chewy texture, and sweet vanilla flavor, these wreaths are sure to become a new Christmas tradition. They're an especially big hit with kids!

YIELD: 13–14 WREATHS

INGREDIENTS:
- 3 Tbsp. (42 g) vegan butter or margarine
- ½ c. (119 ml) brown rice syrup + more for "glue"
- 2 Tbsp. (30 ml) maple syrup
- ¼ c. + 2 Tbsp. (86 g) granulated sugar
- ½ tsp. salt
- 1 tsp. vanilla extract
- 12 drops green food coloring, plus more as needed
- 4 c. (120 g) corn flake cereal
- 1–2 Tbsp. oil (for your fingertips)
- 42 vegan red cinnamon candies*
- Powdered sugar (confectioners' sugar) for dusting

*If you can't find vegan red cinnamon candies, use three dots of red frosting to create your berries instead.

FOR BEST GLUTEN-FREE VERSION:
This recipe is naturally gluten-free; however, double-check labels on all ingredients to be sure.

INSTRUCTIONS:
1. Line two baking sheets with parchment paper and set aside.
2. Melt the butter in a large pot over medium heat.
3. Add the brown rice syrup, maple syrup, sugar, and salt, and cook, stirring frequently, for 3–4 minutes, until slightly thickened.
4. Turn off the heat and remove the pot from the burner, then stir in the vanilla and 12 drops of the food coloring.
5. Add the cereal and stir until the corn flakes are evenly coated. Add more green coloring if needed and stir well again.
6. Using a ¼ cup measuring cup, form and drop mounds onto your baking sheets. Work fairly quickly as the wreaths may start to set and harden.
7. Pour oil into a bowl and oil your fingertips. Then use your fingers to create a hole in the center of each mound and shape it into a wreath. Re-oil your fingertips as needed.
8. Apply 3 small dabs of brown rice syrup in a cluster to each wreath (I use a toothpick or the tip of a spoon). Top with 3 cinnamon candies to create your holly berries. If using red frosting instead, skip the brown rice syrup glue and wait to apply frosting until after the powdered sugar has been added (see next step.)
9. Using a sieve or sifter, dust each wreath with powdered sugar, or sprinkle it on using clean and dry fingertips.
10. Use your fingertips or a slightly dampened paper towel to wipe most of the powdered sugar off the holly berries. If using frosting for the berries, add a cluster of three dots to each wreath now.
11. Let your wreaths sit on the counter for 1–2 hours to harden.

NOTES:
- While your cereal wreaths are setting, check on them every so often to see if they need to be reshaped. Sometimes both the cereal and the cinnamon candies can slide a bit. If they have, simply reshape the leaves or slide the candies back into place.
- Use a minimal amount of brown rice syrup glue for the holly berries. Excess syrup can drip and discolor the green leaves. If this does happen, however, you can usually cover it up with more powdered sugar once it dries.

STORAGE:
These wreaths are flexible and can be stored in airtight containers or non-airtight containers, tins, or on plates covered in foil or plastic wrap.

PEANUT BUTTER BEARS

These soft peanut butter cookie bears make an adorable addition to cookie tins, platters, and party spreads alike. But as cute and sweet peanut buttery delicious as they are, they're even more fun to make! This is truly one of the best cookie recipes to make with the younger bakers in the house, as they love getting creative when shaping the dough and applying the little bear faces.

YIELD: 8–9 BEARS

INGREDIENTS:

- ¾ c. (191 g) smooth all-natural peanut butter
- ½ c. (119 ml) maple syrup + about 1 tsp. (5 ml) for ear "glue"
- ½ c. (70 g) all-purpose flour or ½ c. (60 g) garbanzo bean (chickpea) flour + more as needed
- ½ tsp. salt
- 2 Tbsp. (29 g) granulated sugar for rolling
- 8-9 regular-sized dairy-free chocolate chips and 16-18 dairy-free mini chocolate chips

FOR BEST GLUTEN-FREE VERSION:

If you use garbanzo bean (chickpea) flour, this recipe is naturally gluten-free; however, double-check labels on all ingredients to be sure.

INSTRUCTIONS:

1. Preheat your oven to 350°F (approx. 177°C).
2. In a bowl, combine the peanut butter, maple syrup, flour, and salt and stir well to combine.
3. Pick up a small amount of dough. If it easily rolls into a ball, then you're good to go. If the dough is too loose, add additional flour 1 Tbsp. at a time, stirring in between additions, until it's thick enough to create balls.
4. Place the granulated sugar in a small bowl and keep it close by. Place 1 tsp. of maple syrup in a separate small bowl and keep that close by, as well.
5. To create each bear, roll 1 ½ Tbsp. (30 g) of dough into a ball to make the head, 1 tsp. (6 g) of dough for the muzzle, and ½ tsp. (3 g) of dough for each ear. After creating each ball, roll it in the bowl of sugar to lightly coat, then slightly flatten each ball into a disc shape.
6. To assemble, place the bear head on a parchment-lined or ungreased baking sheet. Add the muzzle to the lower half of the head. Dip one edge of each ear in maple syrup. Using the syrup as "glue," attach the ears to the top of the head. Press carefully so they are sure to stick to the head while baking.
7. Finally, add the nose and eyes. Use 1 regular-sized chocolate chip for the nose, placing it on top of the muzzle. Place 2 mini chocolate chips just above the muzzle on the head for the eyes. Repeat with the remaining dough, syrup, and chocolate chips.
8. Bake in your preheated oven for 9–10 minutes or just until set.
9. Allow the bears to cool on the baking sheet for 2–5 minutes before carefully transferring to a cooling rack.

NOTE:

If you can't find mini chocolate chips, any small, round, dark-colored candy will do.

STORAGE:

These peanut butter bears are flexible and can be stored in airtight or non-airtight containers, tins, or on plates covered with foil or plastic wrap.

MINT COOKIE CHEESECAKE TRUFFLES

These truffles are little bites of sweet, minty cookie magic with a hint of tang and salt, thanks to the cream cheese. They are truly the epitome of minty chocolate deliciousness!

YIELD: **30–33 BITE-SIZED TRUFFLES**

INGREDIENTS:

- 15 mint-flavored chocolate sandwich cookies (or regular chocolate sandwich cookies plus ½ tsp. peppermint extract or mint flavoring)
- ¼–½ c. (57 - 113 g) vegan cream cheese, slightly softened
- 1 c. (approx. 186 g) dairy-free chocolate chips or chopped chocolate bar
- ½–1 tsp. coconut oil (if needed)

FOR BEST GLUTEN-FREE VERSION:
Use gluten-free chocolate sandwich cookies instead of regular. Check the labels for all remaining ingredients to ensure they're gluten-free, as well.

INSTRUCTIONS:

1. Place the cookies in a food processor and blend until crumbly. No food processor? Simply place the cookies in a large resealable plastic storage bag and press all the air out before sealing. Using a mallet, rolling pin, or your fist, smash the cookies until all pieces are pea-sized or smaller. If adding peppermint extract, add it now and blend again.

2. Add just half of the slightly softened cream cheese to the food processor. Pulse to combine. Some vegan cream cheeses contain a higher water content, so you may be fine using just the ¼ c. (57 g.) cream cheese. However, if the mixture seems too dry, add up to ¼ c. (57 g.) more cream cheese and stir well again.

3. Use a ½-Tbsp. / no. 100 (12g) scoop, create 30–33 truffle balls, placing them each 2 inches (5 cm) apart on parchment-lined baking sheets.

4. Place the truffles in your freezer for 20–30 minutes.

5. Once your truffles are sturdy and firm, start melting the chocolate in 30-second increments (stirring in between) in the microwave, or in a double boiler over medium heat. If your chocolate is not velvety-smooth once melted or is too thick to work with, add the coconut oil a little at a time until you reach the desired consistency.

6. Using one spoon in each hand, transfer each truffle ball to the bowl of chocolate and use the spoons to completely coat it with chocolate. Then transfer the ball back to the baking sheet. Note: do your best to use only the spoons for this process and not your fingers, otherwise things will get very messy!

7. If you'd like to sprinkle the surfaces with sprinkles, colored sugar, or a pinch of additional crumbled cookie, do so immediately before the chocolate starts to harden.

8. Allow your truffles to set at room temperature for 2–3 hours.

STORAGE:
Store the truffles at room temperature in non-airtight tins or boxes or on a foil-covered plate. Avoid airtight containers and plastic wrap, as they may cause the truffles to become overly soft.

COCOAS, LATTES, AND TOPPINGS

CLASSIC HOT COCOA

Whether you're cozying up in PJs and a blanket by the fire, heading out for an evening drive to look at Christmas lights, or snuggling on the couch to watch Christmas movies, there's nothing quite like a mug filled with hot cocoa to make a holiday moment feel extra special.

YIELD: 2 SERVINGS

INGREDIENTS:

- 2 c. (474 ml) non-dairy milk
- 3 Tbsp. (35 g) dairy-free chocolate chips or chopped chocolate bar
- 2 Tbsp. (29 g) granulated sugar
- 1 Tbsp. (5 g) cocoa powder
- ¼ tsp. vanilla extract
- ⅛ tsp. salt

INSTRUCTIONS:

1. Warm the milk in a saucepan over medium-high heat until steamy.
2. Whisk in the remaining ingredients until the cocoa powder is dissolved and the chocolate chips are melted.
3. Serve with marshmallows or whipped cream, if you like!

NOTES:

- Do not walk away from the milk warming on the stove, as it may boil over if it gets too hot.
- For richer hot cocoa, add 1 extra tablespoon each cocoa powder and chocolate chips.

PEPPERMINT HOT COCOA

Peppermint and chocolate come together in a heavenly combination to create this fresh and fun take on hot cocoa. Our family especially loves it garnished with cool whipped cream and chopped candy cane pieces.

YIELD: 2 SERVINGS

INGREDIENTS:

- 2 c. (474 ml) non-dairy milk
- 3 Tbsp. (35 g) dairy-free chocolate chips or chopped chocolate bar
- 2 Tbsp. (10 g) cocoa powder
- 2 Tbsp. (29 g) granulated sugar
- ¼–½ tsp. peppermint extract
- ¼ tsp. vanilla extract
- Pinch of salt

INSTRUCTIONS:

1. In asaucepan over medium heat, warm the milk until steamy, 3–5 minutes.

2. Add all the remaining ingredients and whisk until the chocolate chips have melted. When it comes to measuring your peppermint extract, ¼ tsp. will give you a light and fresh mint flavor, whereas ½ tsp. will take you to full candy cane mode! I recommend starting with ¼ tsp. and adding more if desired.

3. Top with marshmallows or whipped cream, if you like!

NOTES:

- Do not walk away from the milk warming on the stove, as it may boil over if it gets too hot.
- For a richer chocolate flavor, add an extra tablespoon of cocoa powder and/or chocolate chips.
- Create Peppermint Mochas by adding 1 ½ tsp. instant coffee or espresso crystals, or by adding 2 shots of fresh espresso.

SALTED CARAMEL HOT COCOA

This luxurious salted caramel hot cocoa is just as marvelous as it sounds. It's velvety, silky smooth, and richly flavored with both caramel and chocolate. This is our favorite drink to enjoy on Christmas Eve as we hang our stockings and gaze at our decorated tree one last time before the big day.

YIELD: 2 SERVINGS

INGREDIENTS:
- ¾ c. (173 g) granulated sugar
- ¼ tsp. lemon juice
- 2 c. (474 ml) non-dairy milk, lukewarm or room temperature
- 3 Tbsp. (35 g) dairy-free chocolate chips, chunks, or chopped chocolate bar
- 1 Tbsp. (5 g) cocoa powder
- ⅛ tsp. salt + more to taste

INSTRUCTIONS:
1. Place a medium saucepan over medium-high heat and allow it to preheat for several minutes until piping hot.
2. Meanwhile, combine the sugar and lemon juice in a bowl and rub the two together until the sugar is damp and fragrant.
3. Once the saucepan is hot, add the sugar, immediately turn the heat down to medium, and start stirring. The sugar will begin to liquefy and take on color. *Note: The sugar may stick to the spoon a bit, but that's okay, do not try to remove it!* Continue stirring until the liquid sugar takes on a medium amber color. Once it reaches this stage, start adding the room-temperature milk approximately ¼–½ c. (59–119 ml) at a time, stirring in between additions. Be cautious, as the milk may create a lot of steam and bubbles. The caramel will likely seize, but that's okay; any hard pieces will melt and become smooth as the milk gets hotter.
4. Once the caramel milk starts to simmer, add the chocolate chips, cocoa powder, and salt and whisk until all the chocolate is melted.
5. Serve with whipped cream, marshmallows, and/or a drizzle of store-bought vegan caramel, if you like!

NOTE:
If not enjoying right away, this cocoa can be kept in the fridge for about 1 week. Reheat before serving.

PUMPKIN SPICED LATTES

A winter latte list wouldn't feel complete if it didn't include the famous drink that started the pumpkin spice craze! Made with real pumpkin and a blend of warming spices, this recipe never disappoints. I love sipping on this latte as I take down the fall decorations and replace them with bright red and green Christmas ones, usually on the Saturday after Thanksgiving.

YIELD: **2 SERVINGS**

INGREDIENTS:
- 1 ½ c. (355 ml) non-dairy milk
- ½ c. (119 ml) canned full-fat coconut milk or other high-fat non-dairy milk
- 2 Tbsp. + 2 tsp. (39 g) granulated sugar
- 2 Tbsp. (30 g) canned pumpkin
- 2 ½ tsp. pumpkin pie spice
- 1 ½ tsp. instant coffee or espresso crystals, or 2 shots of fresh espresso
- Pinch of salt

INSTRUCTIONS:
1. Combine all the ingredients in a medium saucepan and warm over medium heat, whisking frequently, until the desired temperature is reached.
2. Pour into mugs and top lattes with whipped cream and a dusting of cinnamon, if you like.

NOTES:
- For a stronger coffee flavor (and more caffeine), add an extra ½ tsp. coffee crystals.
- These lattes go amazingly with maple or cinnamon whipped cream (page 93)!
- If not enjoying right away, lattes can be kept in the fridge for about 1 week. Reheat before serving.

EGGNOG LATTES

As Christmas draws nearer and the weather gets colder, there are two things that are completely necessary: cozy red scarves and steamy winter lattes. This creamy eggnog version warms you from the inside out, bringing a sense of joy and hygge with each and every sip.

YIELD: **2 SERVINGS**

INGREDIENTS:

- 1 c. (237 ml) non-dairy milk
- 1 c. (237 ml) canned full-fat coconut milk or other high-fat non-dairy milk
- 2 Tbsp. + 2 tsp. (35 g) granulated sugar
- 1 ½ tsp. instant coffee or espresso crystals, or 2 shots of fresh espresso
- ½ tsp. vanilla extract
- ¼ tsp. nutmeg
- ⅛ tsp. ground cloves
- ⅛ tsp. turmeric
- Pinch of salt

INSTRUCTIONS:

1. Combine all the ingredients in a medium saucepan and warm over medium heat, whisking frequently until the desired temperature is reached.

2. Pour into mugs and top lattes with whipped cream and a dusting of nutmeg, if you like.

NOTES:

- For a stronger coffee flavor (and more caffeine), add an extra ½ tsp. coffee crystals.

- For frothier lattes, transfer the latte mixture to a standard-sized blender and blend on high for about 30 seconds. Alternatively, you can use an immersion blender.

- If not enjoying right away, lattes can be kept in the fridge for about 1 week. Reheat before serving.

GINGERBREAD LATTES

If you love the idea of combining the flavors of a gingerbread cookie with your morning coffee, then this is a latte you need to try! I recommend sipping this festive drink on Christmas morning while opening presents with the family. (Mix the ingredients a day or two in advance so you don't miss a moment of the fun!)

YIELD: 2 SERVINGS

INGREDIENTS:
- 2 c. (474 ml) non-dairy milk
- 2 Tbsp. + 2 tsp. (35 g) granulated sugar
- 1 ½ tsp. instant coffee crystals or espresso crystals, or 2 shots of fresh espresso
- ¼ tsp. cinnamon
- ¼ tsp. ginger
- ⅛ tsp. ground cloves
- Pinch of salt

INSTRUCTIONS:
1. Combine all the ingredients in a medium saucepan and warm over medium heat, whisking frequently until the desired temperature is reached.
2. Pour into mugs and top lattes with whipped cream, if you like!

NOTES:
- For creamier lattes, replace ½ c. (119 ml) of the non-dairy milk with full-fat canned coconut milk or another high-fat non-dairy milk.
- For a stronger coffee flavor (and more caffeine), add an extra ½ tsp. coffee crystals.
- For frothier lattes, transfer the hot latte mixture to a standard-sized blender and blend on high for 30 seconds. Alternatively, you can use an immersion blender.
- If not enjoying right away, lattes can be kept in the fridge for about 1 week. Reheat before serving.

MINT MATCHA LATTES

These matcha lattes offer a delightfully minty pick-me-up, making them perfect for sipping while out Christmas shopping or at home writing out your holiday cards. (Psst . . . these lattes are amazingly on the healthy side, too!)

YIELD: **2 SERVINGS**

INGREDIENTS:

- 2 c. (474 ml) non-dairy milk, warmed
- 3 Tbsp. (45 ml) maple syrup + more to taste
- 2 tsp. powdered matcha green tea
- 25–27 fresh mint leaves or 2–3 drops of peppermint extract / flavoring + more to taste
- Handful of fresh spinach (optional)*

*Using the spinach creates a nice bright green color. Don't worry—you can't taste it!

INSTRUCTIONS:

1. In a blender, combine the warmed milk, maple syrup, matcha green tea, mint, and spinach, if using.
2. Blend until completely smooth and liquified.
3. Reheat in the microwave or on the stove, if needed. Top with whipped cream, if you like!

NOTE:

If not enjoying right away, lattes can be kept in the fridge for about 1 week. Reheat before serving.

CHAI TEA LATTES

There's just something about a warm, sweet and spiced chai tea latte that puts me in the holiday spirit. My mom and I love filling our Christmas mugs and enjoying these heavenly lattes as we sit down with pen and paper and plan out our family holiday meals.

YIELD: 2 SERVINGS

INGREDIENTS:
- ⅔ c. (158 ml) water
- 3 black tea bags
- 1 ⅓ c. (316 ml) non-dairy milk
- 3 Tbsp. (41 g) packed brown sugar
- 1 tsp. cinnamon
- ½ tsp. allspice
- ¼–½ tsp. ginger*
- ¼ tsp. vanilla extract
- Pinch of salt

*For those sensitive to ginger, use only ¼ tsp. But for traditional-tasting chai tea lattes, use the full ½ tsp.

INSTRUCTIONS:
1. Bring the water to a boil in a small saucepan over medium-high heat.
2. Once the water boils, turn off the heat and add the tea bags. Allow to steep for 5–6 minutes.
3. Remove the tea bags, squeeze as much tea out of them as you can, and discard.
4. Add all the remaining ingredients to the saucepan and return the heat to medium. Whisk until all the ingredients are mostly incorporated and the desired temperature is reached.
5. Pour into mugs and top with whipped cream, if desired.

NOTES:
- For frothier lattes, transfer the latte mixture to a standard-sized blender and blend on high for 30 seconds to 1 minute. Alternatively, you can use an immersion blender.
- If not enjoying right away, lattes can be kept in the fridge for up to 1 week. Reheat before serving.

CLASSIC WHIPPED CREAM

Take your hot cocoas and lattes to the next level by adding a dollop of cool and decadently creamy homemade whipped cream. Don't miss the flavor variations at the bottom of this recipe, as all four versions of this whipped cream are magical.

YIELD: ABOUT 1 ½ CUPS WHIPPED CREAM

INGREDIENTS:
- Two 13.5-oz. / 400-ml cans coconut cream (or four small cans), chilled in the refrigerator for at least 6 hours or overnight.
- ⅔ c. (87 g) powdered sugar (confectioners' sugar)
- ½ tsp. flavoring (optional, see below)

HOW TO MAKE FUN FLAVORED WHIPPED CREAMS:

- Maple whipped cream: add ½ tsp. maple extract or flavoring
- Peppermint whipped cream: add ½ tsp. peppermint extract
- Cinnamon whipped cream: add a scant ½ tsp. cinnamon

INSTRUCTIONS:
1. Remove the coconut cream from the fridge and scoop out 1 ¼ c. (276 g) of the thick coconut cream from the top. Avoid the watery liquid as much as you can. Place the cream in a mixing bowl. Note: you may only need to open one can.
2. Add the powdered sugar and any flavoring, if using.
3. Using a handheld or stand mixer, mix on medium-low until smooth and fluffy.
4. For slightly thicker whipped cream, place in the freezer for 15 minutes or in the refrigerator for at least 1 hour or overnight.

NOTES:
- This whipped cream is thick and surprisingly heavy in weight, so leave an extra inch (about 3 cm) at the top of your mug, otherwise your drinks may overflow when you add the whipped cream.
- Give your whipped cream more of an ice cream texture by placing it in the freezer for at least 2 hours. Allow it to sit at room temperature for 10 minutes before serving.
- It's usually best to chill one extra can of coconut cream for backup, as every once in a great while, you'll end up with coconut cream that doesn't set when chilled.

STORAGE:
This whipped cream can be made in advance and stored in the fridge for about 2 weeks or in the freezer for 1 month. Thaw frozen whipped cream at room temperature for 20 minutes or in the refrigerator for several hours before serving.

HOMEMADE MARSHMALLOWS

If you really want to impress your family and friends, do so by serving a batch of fresh homemade marshmallows at your hot cocoa bar this Christmas. They're soft, sweet, and pillowy, adding the perfect special touch to any hot drink—and of course, they're also really fun to eat all on their own!

YIELD: 49 MARSHMALLOWS

INGREDIENTS:
- vegan butter or margarine for greasing
- ⅓–½ c. (43–65 g) powdered sugar (confectioners' sugar) for dusting
- ⅓ c. (79 ml) aquafaba (the liquid in a can of chickpeas / garbanzo beans, ideally low or no sodium)
- ¼ tsp. cream of tartar
- 2 Tbsp. (30 ml) vanilla extract
- ½ c. + 1 Tbsp. (133 ml) water
- 1 Tbsp. (8 g) agar powder (not flakes)
- 1 c. (288 g) granulated sugar

FOR BEST GLUTEN-FREE VERSION:
This recipe should be naturally gluten-free; however, double-check all ingredient labels to be sure.

STORAGE:
Store the marshmallows in airtight containers away from heat.

> **For peppermint marshmallows:**
> Reduce the vanilla extract to 1 Tbsp. + 1 tsp. (20 ml) and add ½ tsp. peppermint extract.

INSTRUCTIONS

1. Lightly grease the sides and bottom of an 8-x-8-inch (20-x-20-cm) square baking dish with butter. Then, lightly dust with 1 Tbsp. or less of powdered sugar. Set aside.

2. Using a handheld or stand mixer with a whisk attachment, whip the aquafaba and cream of tartar on the highest speed possible for 7–9 minutes. It will become very white and fluffy.

3. Add the vanilla extract and whip for 1–3 minutes more, until it turns white again and stiff peaks form. Scrape the sides of the bowl as needed.

4. In a small saucepan, combine the water and agar powder and bring to a boil over medium heat. Boil, stirring constantly, for 2–3 minutes, then add the granulated sugar and cook for 3 minutes more, continuing to stir constantly. Lower the heat to medium-low, if it looks as though it may overflow. When the mixture becomes very bubbly and foamy and a deep golden color, or registers 215°F (about 102°C) on a candy thermometer, turn off the heat.

5. Begin mixing the aquafaba mixture again on low speed, then slowly add the hot sugar mixture to the aquafaba. Do not scrape the gel from the sides or bottom of the saucepan as you do this; only add what easily comes out on its own, otherwise you may have lumpy marshmallows. Mix for about 30 seconds; the mixture will be fluffy and slightly shiny. Turn off the mixer and gently fold the marshmallow mixture a few times using a rubber spatula to ensure none of the liquid sugar has pooled at the bottom of the bowl.

6. Quickly pour the mixture into the prepared baking dish. Dust the top of the marshmallows with powdered sugar, then allow to sit on a cooling rack for at least 2 hours.

7. Using a sharp knife, cut into 1-inch (2.5-cm) squares, then carefully remove the marshmallows several at time using a thin, flat spatula. Transfer to a baking sheet. Separate the marshmallows from one another and allow them to dry out a bit for 3–4 hours. For quicker drying, heat your oven to 150°F (66°C). Once it reaches that temperature, turn off the heat and place the baking sheet of marshmallows in the oven for 1 hour.

NOTE:
- Just before serving, pile marshmallows on a plate and dust with a little extra powdered sugar.

INDEX

RAVE REVIEWS FOR VEGAN CHRISTMAS COOKIES & COCOA:

Named one of VegNews's Top 10 Vegan Cookbooks of the Holiday Season (2020)

AMAZON

"This is the best vegan baking cookbook ever! This book is full of yummy, decadent vegan recipes everyone will love, and non-vegans won't have a clue the tasty treats are egg- and dairy-free. The recipes are easy to follow and the photos are beautiful, so you know what the finished product looks like. I found out about the cookbook at audreydunham.com, where I found a ton of shortcuts and healthy recipes that really taste good! Totally worth the money."

"Exactly what I was looking for! Delicious and vegan!"

"Super easy, healthy, and delish! Highly recommend!"

GOOD READS

"Delicious vegan cookie and bar recipes for a year-round sugar rush. Vegan versions of classic Christmas cookies like Linzer Cookies, Spritz Cookies, Peppermint Pinwheels, and more. Excited to try the Salted Caramel Turtle Cookie, Pecan Pie Bar, and Red Velvet Crinkle Cookie recipes."

ABOUT THE AUTHOR

Audrey Dunham is a vegan recipe creator who shares quick and easy yet super flavorful recipes on her website, AudreyDunham.com, as well as on her YouTube channel, YouTube.com/AudreyDunham. She is the founder and creator of Peanut's Bake Shop Cookie Kits (decadent vegan and gluten-free cookie mixes), proud wife to comedian and ventriloquist Jeff Dunham, mama to twin boys, and step-mama to three grown girls.

Audrey loves holidays and *loves* baking Christmas cookies, especially if it's with her young twin boys, Jack and James, at their home in Los Angeles, CA.

After going the vegan route, Audrey refused to say farewell to all of her childhood cookie favorites. Instead, she "veganized" those recipes and put them all in this cookbook for others to enjoy as well. With so many needing or choosing a dairy-free, egg-free, or vegan diet, Audrey's goal is to create recipes that are just as good as (if not better than!) the traditional versions.

To connect with Audrey, you can find her on these social platforms:

Instagram: @AudreyDunham
Facebook: Audrey Dunham